DRAMA CLASSICS

BEHN

THE

ROVER

D0046969

DRAMA CLASSICS

The Drama Classics series aims to offer the world's greatest plays in affordable paperback editions for students, actors and theatregoers. The hallmarks of the series are accessible introductions, uncluttered texts and an overall theatrical perspective.

Given that readers may be encountering a particular play for the first time, the introduction seeks to fill in the theatrical/historical background and to outline the chief themes rather than concentrate on interpretational and textual analysis. Similarly the play-texts themselves are free of footnotes and other interpolations: instead there is an end-glossary of 'difficult' words and phrases.

The texts of the English-language plays in the series have been prepared taking full account of all existing scholarship. The foreign-language plays have been newly translated into a modern English that is both actable and accurate: many of the translators regularly have their work staged professionally.

Edited until his early death by Kenneth McLeish, the Drama Classics series continues with his aim of providing a first-class library of dramatic literature representing the best of world theatre.

Associate editors:
Professor Trevor R. Griffiths
*Visiting Professor in Humanities, Universities of Essex and
 Hertfordshire*
Dr Colin Counsell
*School of Humanities, Arts and Languages,
 London Metropolitan University*

DRAMA CLASSICS *the first hundred*

The Alchemist
All for Love
Andromache
Antigone
Bacchae
Bartholomew Fair
The Beaux Stratagem
The Beggar's Opera
Birds
Blood Wedding
Celestina
The Changeling
A Chaste Maid in Cheapside
The Cherry Orchard
Children of the Sun
El Cid
The Country Wife
The Dance of Death
The Devil is an Ass
Doctor Faustus
A Doll's House
Don Juan
The Duchess of Malfi
Edward II
Electra (Euripides)
Electra (Sophocles)
An Enemy of the People
Everyman
Faust
A Flea in her Ear
Frogs
Fuente Ovejuna
The Game of Love and Chance
Ghosts
The Government Inspector
Hecuba
Hedda Gabler

The Hypochondriac
The Importance of Being Earnest
An Ideal Husband
An Italian Straw Hat
Ivanov
The Jew of Malta
The Knight of the Burning Pestle
The Lady from the Sea
The Learned Ladies
Lady Windermere's Fan
Life is a Dream
London Assurance
The Lower Depths
The Lucky Chance
Lulu
Lysistrata
The Malcontent
The Man of Mode
The Marriage of Figaro
Mary Stuart
The Master Builder
Medea
The Misanthrope
The Miser
Miss Julie
A Month in the Country
Oedipus
The Oresteia
Peer Gynt
Phedra
The Playboy of the Western World
The Recruiting Officer
The Revenger's Tragedy
The Rivals

The Roaring Girl
La Ronde
Rosmersholm
The Rover
Scapino
The School for Scandal
The Seagull
The Servant of Two Masters
She Stoops to Conquer
The Shoemakers' Holiday
Six Characters in Search of an Author
The Spanish Tragedy
Spring Awakening
Summerfolk
Tartuffe
Three Sisters
'Tis Pity She's a Whore
Too Clever by Half
Ubu
Uncle Vanya
Volpone
The Way of the World
The White Devil
The Wild Duck
A Woman of No Importance
Women Beware Women
Women of Troy
Woyzeck
Yerma

The publishers welcome suggestions for further titles

DRAMA CLASSICS

THE ROVER

by

Aphra Behn

edited and with an introduction by
Simon Trussler

NICK HERN BOOKS

London
www.nickhernbooks.demon.co.uk

A Drama Classic

This edition of *The Rover* first published in Great Britain
as a paperback original in 1999 by Nick Hern Books Limited,
The Glasshouse, 49a Goldhawk Road, London W12 8QP

Reprinted 2002, 2007, 2010, 2011, 2013

Typeset by Country Setting, Kingsdown, Kent CT14 8ES
Printed in the UK by Mimeo Ltd, Huntingdon, Cambridgeshire
PE29 6XX

A CIP catalogue record for this book is available from
the British Library

ISBN 978 1 85459 178 4

Woodland
CARBON
www.woodlandcarbon.co.uk
NICK HERN BOOKS
Printed on Carbon Captured paper

Introduction

Aphra Behn (1640–1689)

Aphra Behn is thought to have been born near Canterbury, in Kent, in the summer of 1640. In her early twenties her father was appointed Lieutenant-General of the then British colony of Surinam, in South America, but died on the voyage out to the Guianas. She stayed long enough to absorb the experiences which were later to shape her novel *Oronooko* but returned home to England in the spring of 1664. Within a year she was married to Mr Behn – an elusive figure, possibly a Dutch merchant with Guianese connections, who died soon afterwards, perhaps during the Great Plague of 1665. One of the managers of London's two theatre companies, Thomas Killigrew, an intimate of the recently restored King, Charles II, was evidently instrumental in Aphra Behn being briefly employed as a spy during the Dutch wars (which saw Surinam ceded to the Netherlands), but by 1667 she was again in London – and in the following year was imprisoned for debt, despite Killigrew's intercession on her behalf.

Until she reached the age of thirty, Behn's life is thus as full of false starts and uncertainties for the would-be biographer as it must have seemed to the woman herself. In that year, however, she not only established her career as a playwright – with a tragi-comedy called *The Forced Marriage*, which enjoyed a moderate success at the theatre in Lincoln's Inn Fields – but began a relationship with the dissolute lawyer John Hoyle, one of several supposed originals for Willmore in *The Rover*. For the following twelve years she became a fully professional playwright – an exceptional career for a woman at that time – writing some twenty plays, most of them comedies for the new Dorset Garden Theatre.

By the early 1680s, however, fashionable London was becoming more preoccupied with politics than with theatre. The then emerging Whig and Tory factions were at odds over the right of the King's Catholic brother, James, to succeed to the throne in the event of Charles remaining without a legitimate heir. In 1682 Aphra Behn contributed an allegedly 'abusive' and 'scandalous' prologue to an anonymous anti-Whig play, and found herself again under arrest. She was let off with a caution, but thereafter turned increasingly to the safer forms of fiction and poetry – though she enjoyed a final stage triumph in 1687 with a highly original, *commedia*-style farce, *The Emperor of the Moon*, before publishing what was for long her best-known work, the novel *Oronooko*, in 1688. The death of Charles in the same year, and the 'Bloodless Revolution' which saw off the hapless James, marked the end of the world Aphra Behn had known, and she died the following April, just before her forty-ninth birthday.

What Happens in the Play

'The rover' is the philandering cavalier Willmore, a seafaring adventurer who meets up in Naples with fellow exiles from Cromwell's rule, the mercenary soldiers Belvile and Frederick, and the rustic 'gull', the easily deceived simpleton Ned Blunt. The Neapolitan beauty Florinda is in love with Belvile, despite being intended by her father for an elderly suitor, and by her brother Don Pedro for his own friend, the viceroy's son Don Antonio. Her younger sister, the sprightly Hellena, is no less reluctantly meant for a nun. The festivities of the pre-Lenten carnival are just getting under way, and with their cousin, the demure but calculating Valeria, the girls plan to disguise themselves as gypsies, join in the celebrations – and look out for men.

Antonio and Pedro fall out over the charms of the courtesan Angellica Bianca, who is demanding an outrageous sum for her favours; but she is eventually seduced into giving them freely to the flamboyant but impoverished Willmore – of whom she becomes wildly jealous when she later catches him paying court to Hellena in her gypsy disguise. Florinda has meanwhile arranged a midnight meeting with Belvile at her garden gate, but before his arrival she is accosted by the drunken Willmore, who disturbs the whole house.

As Belvile reproaches his friend, they observe Antonio about to enter Angellica's house, and Willmore wounds his rival – but it is Belvile who is arrested. Brought before Don Antonio, Belvile agrees to stand in for him in the duel planned with Don Pedro. Belvile almost gets possession of his mistress as a result, but is yet again thwarted by the untimely arrival of Willmore.

Hellena now fans the flames of jealousy between Angellica and Willmore, while Florinda, fleeing from her brother, finds herself in the hands of Ned Blunt – intent on avenging himself against womanhood for the trick by which the prostitute Lucetta has deprived him of his possessions and his dignity. But his friends arrive in time to prevent a rape, Florinda's true identity is revealed, and she and Belvile secure a priest to marry them. Valeria and her beau Frederick also take advantage of the priest's services. Willmore is rescued by Antonio from death at the hands of the vengeful Angellica, but submits to marriage at the hands of Hellena. Don Pedro reluctantly resigns himself to events.

Sources and Stage History

In the postscript to *The Rover* (page 123), Aphra Behn feels it necessary to defend herself against charges of plagiarism: but she made no secret of her debt to Thomas Killigrew's earlier play *Thomaso; or, The Wanderer*. This had been written in 1654, without any expectation of performance – the theatres having been closed since the outbreak of the civil wars – and was published in Killigrew's *Comedies and Tragedies* ten years later. Behn claims that she might as well be accused of taking her ideas from Richard Brome's *The Novella*, first performed in 1632: but whereas she borrowed from Brome only in minor matters of construction, and perhaps for a faint original of Angellica, *The Rover* is clearly obliged to Killigrew's play in its general plot outline, and there are clear stylistic echoes. However, a comparison of her Willmore and Ned Blunt with Killigrew's counterparts, Thomaso and Edwardo, shows how far her skill in characterization transcends her source, just as she is superior to the prolix Killigrew in sustaining the dramatic pace and in the tightness of her plot construction.

Like so many of Aphra Behn's plays, *The Rover* was written for the Dorset Garden Theatre, which had opened with Thomas Betterton as joint manager in 1671. At the first recorded performance, on 24 March 1677, Charles II was present to see Betterton take the role of Belvile, with his wife Mary as Florinda. Betterton's friend, the versatile actor William Smith, played Willmore, and the brilliant low comedian Cave Underhill took the part of Ned Blunt. Elizabeth Barry, who was to become better known for her tragic roles, played Hellena.

Although the play was revived every few years until the turn of the century, it was in the first half of the eighteenth century that it became firmly established in the repertoire, from which it was absent for only a single season between 1703 and 1743. Following in the footsteps of Will Mountfort's Willmore – 'dangerous to see', according to Queen Mary, because 'he made vice so alluring' – Robert Wilks often took the role early in the new century. Mrs Barry had graduated to Angellica by 1707. A revival at Covent Garden in 1757, with Ned Shuter an outstanding Blunt, led to further productions in the following four seasons, but the play then disappeared from the repertoire until 1790, when a bowdlerisation entitled *Love in Many Masks* was put together by Kemble for Drury Lane. The changing moral climate which necessitated this treatment explains why the stage history of *The Rover* was then interrupted for the best part of two centuries.

When, at last, the play was restored to the stage, under the direction of John Barton at the Royal Shakespeare Company's new Swan Theatre in 1986, Barton felt it needful to revise the text, incorporating material of his own along with lines from Killigew's *Thomaso*, and to reshape the structure (which he described as 'hazy and loose in places') to clarify an otherwise 'confusing' plot. His adaptation had the great merit – along with a slightly earlier revival of *The Lucky Chance* at the Royal Court – of reclaiming a rightful place for Aphra Behn among her acknowledged Restoration contemporaries: but subsequent revivals have effortlessly reverted to Behn's text, suggesting that her plotting is neither more nor less complicated than theirs (or Shakespeare's, for that matter), just less familiar. And where Barton's production had, consciously or otherwise, glossed over the play's darker side in favour of swaggering comedy, later productions have more openly addressed Willmore's abuse of women and his friends' casual contemplation of rape, blending comedy with ambiguity in an appropriate and challenging mix.

The Return of the Banished Cavaliers

The events which restored Charles II to the English throne in May 1660 were fast-moving: as late as September 1659, both Charles and his brother James had appeared to be making plans for an indefinite exile. Much had to be done during the new king's 'honeymoon' with his people, and it is a measure of the importance attached by Charles to theatrical matters that he seems to have given as much urgent attention to sorting out the squabbles between the various entrepreneurs vying to form new theatrical companies as to reconciling the old enemies of the civil wars.

After his apparently final defeat at Worcester in 1651, exile for Charles had been a relatively comfortable affair, passed mainly in the civilised if often conspiratorial surroundings of Paris and Brussels: but for many of the followers of the king and his 'martyred' father, the interregnum was spent in a constant struggle against hardship. Some laid low at home, their estates confiscated or sold off piecemeal to meet fines for their 'delinquency'. Others, like Belvile and Willmore in *The Rover*, became soldiers or sailors of fortune, accumulating mistresses, booty, or battle honours with equally offhand loyalty.

Most of the young Restoration gallants, now returning to England along with their king, would thus in all probability have spent a childhood or adolescence in the turbulent atmosphere of civil war, the early years of their adult life cut off from both family traditions and the sense of service which possession of land could still, on occasion, instil. Nor did the compromise between the old and new interests we call the 'Restoration settlement' return the estates sold off by persecuted royalists to puritan land-grabbers. Lacking roots, but often bearing a load of such grudges, these 'rovers' saw little reason not to pursue in England the kind of sexual and economic opportunism which had ruled their life-style in exile. Such opportunism was duly reflected in the plays they watched and wrote.

Besides, there was even a sort of moral justification for living out the belief that 'debauchery was loyalty, gravity rebellion': for inverting the detested values of puritanism was surely to be commended. And an open delight in sexual dalliance (as in theatricality) happily coincided with the tastes of the restored monarch. No wonder that Charles's court in Whitehall proved such a magnet, and that its values permeated the life and attitudes of 'the town' – the residential and shopping area of the fashionable West End, of which Covent Garden was then the youthful heart and the Strand the main artery.

By contrast, 'the city' was the City of London, further east, whose tradesmen and financiers, tainted with puritan sympathies, became the 'cits' so often mocked in the prologues, epilogues and cuckoldings of Restoration comedy. That the king, no less than his courtiers, was often dependent on the financial assistance of these worthies made it, of course, all the more necessary to display them as semi-illiterate upstarts in the theatre – which the 'cits' none the less attended, sometimes in such numbers as to spoil Samuel Pepys's enjoyment. In the 'party' system now for the first time emerging in British politics, it was from the 'cits' and the interests of money that the Whigs drew their main strength, with the 'Tories' representing the more traditional and largely rural interests of 'land'.

The tensions of a nation and a capital which remained so divided were reflected in its theatre. Although the setting of *The Rover* is one of exile in a faraway country, its values are those of men restored to their country, but not to their own. Thus, the thwarting of an aged father's wish to marry his daughter to a rich but geriatric suitor is an age-old theme of comedy: but whereas the contemporary *commedia* made prominent characters of its Pantaloons and their doddering friends, it is significant that Behn keeps Florinda's stern father and the dyspeptic Don Vincentio permanently off-stage. The traditional struggles between the values of youth and age, poverty and wealth, give way here to just the kind of inter-necine sexual warfare through which the 'banished cavaliers' of real life continued to drown – or to sublimate – their sorrows.

The King, the Court, and the Courtesans

The character of Charles II might very easily have been conceived as the hero of a Wycherley play – dour, cynical, and introverted at heart, yet capable of a pretty wit, and sexually attractive beyond the advantages of *force majeure*. Whether his personality was shaped by exile, or simply well adapted to it, the fact remains that, before the Restoration, Charles enjoyed the semblance of both power and responsibility without the reality of either: life became, in short, a form of play-acting.

Later, when the king strolled, supposedly incognito but recognised by all, into the House of Lords to listen to a debate, he would declare the entertainment as good as a play, and sardonically join in the laughter at veiled references to himself.

In exile, Charles had pursued his women with no less fervour then Willmore in *The Rover* – choosing his mistresses from among his own camp-followers, the nobility of the French court, or the brothels of Paris with the impartiality of a glutton for sex rather than a connoisseur of beauty. Back home, Charles's male companions were drawn largely from a promiscuous, hard-drinking, but highly literate set which included, besides the notorious Earl of Rochester, the Duke of Buckingham, Sir George Etherege and Charles Sedley – all playwrights, as much probably from fashion as inclination, just as in other ages courtiers might have been concerned to excel at hunting deer, jousting, or grouse-shooting.

These were men to whom casual violence came readily, and who trod with equanimity that uneasy tightrope between rape and seduction, between brutality and the defence of honour, which is so often reflected in the plays they wrote and watched. A regular attender at the theatres, Charles himself is said to have lent a hand in the writing of plays, and he also interested himself in matters of casting. He both encouraged and emulated the Restoration 'style', in dramatic art as in life – and apparently displayed it as freely among women of good breeding as among his male cronies or his concubines. It made for sexual equality, of a sort.

When the dynastic imperative finally cornered the king into marriage, he took to wife the unfortunate princess Catherine of Braganza – in part to safeguard the alliance with her native Portugal, in part to produce for the nation an unquestionably legitimate heir. This she failed to do – so perpetuating the long drawn-out crisis over the ever-likelier succession of Charles's Catholic brother, James. The king's treatment of his wife in many ways epitomised the double standards of Restoration comedy. In private, he humiliated her by appointing his own mistresses – successively, Barbara Villiers, Countess of Castlemaine, and Louise de Kéroualle, Duchess of Portsmouth – as ladies of her bedchamber. Yet in public he allowed a curious sense of honour to guide his political instinct, and when the Whigs backed Titus Oates's allegations of Catherine's complicity in a plot to poison her husband, they misjudged their man. Charles refused to put away his wife, the allegations collapsed – and the Whigs, by then espousing the cause of Charles's illegitimate son, Monmouth, lost all credibility, along with their hopes of excluding James from the succession.

Aphra Behn flayed the Whigs with impunity in *The City Heiress* in 1682, but when she widened her target to include Monmouth himself, in her prologue to *Romulus and Hersilia* later that year, she was arrested, and at least severely reprimanded. Charles's affection for his unruly bastard son, or some perverse sense of his far-flung family's dignity, never entirely deserted him – nor, of course, did he forget his mistresses, of whom two of the most prominent came from the theatre. Mary Davis he took from the Duke's company, and the almost legendary Nell Gwyn from the King's – where her position was due to real talent and wit as well as to her undoubted beauty. When, at the height of the crisis over the succession to the throne, Nell's coach was mistaken for that of Charles's Catholic mistress, the Duchess of Portsmouth, she famously won over a jostling mob by declaring from the window, 'Pray, good people, be civil. I am the *protestant* whore!' The line displays all the wry, self-aware sexuality of one of Aphra Behn's new women. Aphra and Nell were, in fact, close friends.

Even in death, Charles exhibited something like the last-act repentance of a rake from Restoration comedy: at the prompting of Lady Portsmouth, he was attended by a priest, and made a deathbed conversion to Catholicism – the priest, by a fine irony, taking the covert, backstairs route to his bedchamber well-worn by so many of Charles's mistresses. And among his last words were those of commendation to his brother James: 'Let not poor Nelly starve.' In a room filled with as many illegitimate offspring as could be hastily assembled, neither Nell Gwyn nor any of his other women were permitted to pay their last respects. 'Poor Nelly' died of an apoplexy soon after. There is little in Restoration comedy which exceeds Charles's personal excesses, or typifies better than his own conduct the mixture of calculation and generosity – and, to our sensibility, the sexual double-standards – which cloaked the Restoration 'wit'.

The Altered Face of the Stage

'They altered at once the whole face of the stage by introducing scenes and women' – or so John Dennis claimed nostalgically, writing in 1725 of the events of 1660, when play-acting was once more permitted after being banned by the puritans since 1642. The court masques of the Jacobean and Caroline theatre had employed quite elaborate scenery, and the open-air theatres of the Elizabethans had long been giving way to indoor 'private' theatres, with greater potential for technical effects. The difference now was that the proscenium arch formed a 'picture-frame' for painted perspective scenery, changed by the wings-and-shutters system, which provided a formalised background to Restoration comedy and tragedy.

But it was *only* a background: the actors performed on the extensive apron stage in front of the proscenium, in a relationship with their audiences no less intimate and uncluttered than their forebears. Indeed, Restoration theatres, which seated from around five to eight hundred, were actually smaller than Elizabethan public playhouses, and their audiences, although not drawn quite so exclusively from a courtly elite as has sometimes been suggested, certainly felt themselves to be part of a social as much as a theatrical occasion.

So to an extent did the actors – hence that 'crossing of the boundary' between actor and character so clearly felt in many

Restoration prologues and epilogues, where the player speaks simultaneously in character and in his or her own person. How this affected the acting of the play itself is not certain: but the style would certainly have been presentational rather than realistic – at a time when rituals of 'presentation' were, of course, prominent in everyday behaviour as well. So, with directors unthought of, and playwrights far less involved in the practical business of mounting a play than their Elizabethan counterparts, the influence of the dancing-master was probably strong in matters of movement and stage grouping. As Jocelyn Powell aptly summed it up: 'The atmosphere of the Restoration theatre was that of a sophisticated cabaret.'

Of those managers seeking the 'patents' which would permit them to create theatrical companies amidst the political confusion of Charles's return, the two successful bidders were both men of influence at court, who had had experience of theatre before the civil wars. It was Thomas Killigrew who wrote the play on which Aphra Behn based *The Rover* – but whereas his *Thomaso* had been intended for reading only, Sir William Davenant had even succeeded in getting plays with music produced under Cromwell's guard (opera, like melodrama later, thus originating in England as a means of getting round the law). Davenant was given his royal patent to manage, under the patronage of the Duke of York, a company which first played in a converted 'real' tennis court at Lincoln's Inn Fields – the older theatres having been pulled down or left derelict during the civil wars. They moved in 1671 to a playhouse purpose built by Wren – the Dorset Garden Theatre, beside the Thames, where many of Aphra Behn's plays were performed. Killigrew's company, which came under the king's own patronage, played in another converted tennis court until the first Drury Lane Theatre was completed in 1663 (to be replaced by a new playhouse in 1674 after its destruction by fire).

With just two companies of less than thirty players apiece – reduced to a single 'united' company from 1682 to 1695 –

acting was thus an exclusive though not prestigious profession, its members as well-known personally to many in the audience as their own acquaintances in the pit or boxes. And, although the patents stressed that the introduction of actresses was a matter of morality – to correct the abuse of men appearing 'in the habits of women' – intimacy between these players and their audiences was not confined to closeness in the auditorium. It was probably inevitable that, in the absence of a traditional route for women into the profession, some actresses in a licentious age should have achieved their positions through sexual patronage – though it's also indisputable that Elizabeth Barry, despite her path being smoothed by the notorious rake Lord Rochester, became a truly great tragic actress, while Nell Gwyn, although she owed her early chances to being the mistress of a leading player, Charles Hart, became no less striking a comic actress before she caught the eye of the king.

Other actresses, such as the great Thomas Betterton's wife Mary, were none the less able to lead lives of untainted virtue at a time when such behaviour in courtly society was almost eccentric. The fine comic actress Anne Bracegirdle even managed to sustain a reputation for excessive prudishness in private life. This did not, however, prevent her being thought fair game for predatory males: as late as 1692, an assault on her honour was compounded by the murder of the actor William Mountford, who had tried to intervene on her behalf. Those guilty were not severely punished.

This was an age when Rochester might order Dryden to be beaten up in a back alley for an imagined satirical slight; when the king himself could instigate an assault upon a parliamentarian who had dared to criticise his mistresses; and when Rochester and Sedley could attempt the rape of an heiress in broad daylight. The mixture of violence and casual sexuality which Aphra Behn presents even less discreetly than most of her contemporaries – in Willmore, almost with pride – is thus a reflection on the stage of the very brittle veneer of politeness which barely concealed the viciousness of much high-society life.

The Professionalism of Aphra Behn

Aphra Behn was not the first known woman playwright: that distinction goes to a tenth-century Benedictine nun named Hrotsvitha, who wrote six religious dramas while in the German abbey of Gandersheim. That Hrotsvitha's plays should glorify the virtue of chastity was only to be expected in a period when the typology of women allowed few gradations between the virgin and the whore, other than that of the nagging shrew – but her shadow falls strangely before the women playwrights of the Restoration.

Behn was not quite the earliest of these. Margaret Cavendish, Marchioness of Newcastle, published two collections, including some twenty plays, in 1662 and 1668, but these were never performed. Catherine Phillips, however, achieved the honour of having her *Pompey*, a version of a play by the contemporary French writer Corneille, performed in the brand new Smock Alley Theatre in Dublin in February 1663 – and so of inaugurating the vogue for 'heroic dramas', in the rhymed couplets which were to displace blank verse as the main medium for tragic writing until Buckingham's *The Rehearsal* helped to burlesque heroics off the stage in 1671. Just as Catherine Phillips adopted the pen-name of Orinda, so Aphra Behn also allowed herself to be known as Astraea. But where Phillips had written purely for her own amusement – at a time when most male playwrights were courtiers and men of letters, often unconcerned with the income their plays produced – Behn wrote from pressing financial need.

The theatre of the period differed from Shakespeare's in that most playwrights were not formally attached to a particular company. Dryden's contract to write three plays a year in return for becoming a 'sharer' in the King's company was unusual – and unfulfilled. Generally, the professional writer was dependent upon the benefit system, whereby the profits of the third night's performance – and perhaps of the sixth, and exceptionally of the ninth – were allocated to him. A good benefit could reap as much as £100, with a further lump sum possible for publication: but there was no guarantee that any play would even reach the third night, and it was thus as important that a sympathetic audience should give a rousing reception on the first night as that a rich one (perhaps willing to pay well over the expected price for their seats) should fill the house on the third.

Those males scandalised by Aphra Behn, who dared to affront 'the modesty of her sex' by writing as bawdily as they, did not even deign to consider the element of economic necessity that drove her to satisfy the prevailing tastes of the town. She was among the more prolific of Restoration playwrights in part because she *had* to be – and the total of at least sixteen plays performed during her lifetime is thus in marked contrast with, say, Wycherley's four, or Congreve's six. When she declared in the preface to her late comedy *The Lucky Chance* (1686) that she was 'not content to write for a third night only', she may have been staking a conventional claim to be writing for posterity as well as for money: but her long association with Dorset Garden and the regularity of her output may suggest some more formal financial arrangement with the Duke's company than the chances of the benefit system allowed.

In 1682 the two companies merged, in consequence of the decline in theatre attendances in the wake of the political crises of Charles's later years; and the United Company cut its costs still further by staging a higher proportion of revivals, whose dead authors made no claim upon diminishing receipts. Other playwrights, such as Behn's friends Thomas Otway and William Wycherley, fared no better, and John Dryden was forced to seek meagre government patronage. Classically educated males could at least turn to publishing translations as an alternative source of income – whereas Aphra Behn, in contributing to a version of Ovid, had to work from someone else's draft translation. Greek and Latin were no part of the expected female 'accomplishments'.

Aphra Behn enjoyed renewed stage success in later life – notably with *The Lucky Chance* and the strikingly original *The Emperor of the Moon*. But increasingly – and in not dissimilar circumstances to her eighteenth-century successor, Henry Fielding – she turned from plays to writing novels. In 1688, the year before her death, she published *Oronooko*, the work by which she probably remains best known – its anti-slavery theme anticipating Harriet Beecher Stowe, and its element of noble savagery even foreshadowing Rousseau. Whether or not she was the first 'true' novelist, before such aspirants as Defoe, Richardson and Fielding, depends on one's definition of the novel – a form in which, however, women writers were to overcome assumptions of male supremacy with greater success than (until very recently) they challenged male chauvinism in the theatre.

The Sexual Economics of the Restoration

The 'values of family life' may not have been a Victorian invention, but in most earlier drama and literature little love is expected to be lost between fathers and sons, elder and younger brothers, or even (once trapped in marriage) husbands and wives. The death of a wealthy father or elder brother is usually a matter for congratulation among the friends of the fortunate heir – while marriage, of course, has everything to do with the businesslike arrangement of property and dynasties, and very little to do with the affections. True love, before marriage or after, is reserved for a mistress – though in most romantic comedies, where love is actually permitted to culminate in marriage, the hopeful suitor by luck or judgement usually gets a respectable fortune besides.

In real life, the young couple might not even have met before
their parents or go-betweens had finished arranging the match.
(Ordinary working folk could, ironically, better 'afford' to marry
for love the less they could afford anything else: but, until quite
recently, ordinary working folk have not much figured in great
literature or theatre, other than as comic relief.) And the matter
was further complicated by the 'sexual revolution' which led
Charles I to declare in 1664 that 'the passion of love is very
much out of fashion in this country'. Even the once-adored
mistress was now regarded as for sexual satisfaction only – an
object of that curious combination of arousal and disgust which
permeates the poems of such burnt-out rakes as Rochester.
And the disgust is perhaps most readily heaped on those women
who tried reciprocally to exercise the sexual freedom they had
supposedly been granted.

Aphra Behn herself advocated a liberalised sexuality for women.
But she acknowledged that the lack of an equivalent economic
independence (combined with the fear or actuality of childbirth
and the earlier loss of physical charms) constrained women from
exercising their 'freedom' from a position of any other equality
than that of their wits. And freedom of sexual movement was
not freedom of *social* movement: the over-compliant mistress was
still widely regarded as no better than a whore – to which status
abandonment or decline could all too often reduce her. If
Restoration actresses also called themselves 'Mrs' it was not
because they had all been married, but because 'Miss' had come
to be suggestive merely of sexual availability. Mrs Behn herself
enjoyed the relative independence from male domination that
only widowhood could bring – but not the inherited fortune that
would have added security to freedom.

Aphra Behn was not above evading the problem in her plays –
or rather, not above reconciling it, as many writers had done
and would do again, by such a device as she used in *The Dutch
Lover*, where, for all her heroine's vaunted rebellion against
paternal choice, her preferred lover turns out to be her father's
selected suitor as well. And if the very title of Behn's first play,

The Forced Marriage, anticipates the importance of the theme to her writing, by her second, *The Amorous Prince,* she was falling back on the convention that the most promiscuous rake will assuredly reform when the final curtain looms.

The Town Fop showed the horrific consequences of a forced marriage, from which the participants are only released thanks to the hero's earlier, legally-binding pledge of marriage to his mistress. The father, meanwhile, has had time to see the consequences of his own preference – which include the hero spending half his unwanted wife's portion on a debauch. But no resolution is offered by Behn to the economic and sexual plight of the rejected wife – a 'loose end' not dissimilar to that in *The Rover* of the scorned Angellica, in whom the playwright seems to have invested a considerable, perhaps all too personal passion.

Aphra Behn, then, made no pretence of having resolved, dramatically or personally, all the problems posed by the combination of new attitudes to sexuality with very old attitudes to other kinds of freedom. In many ways she was no less equivocal or downright muddled about sex than most of her male counterparts – though she probably did recognise, as her biographer Angeline Goreau expresses it, that the 'liberated' wits of the Restoration were fearfully if unconsciously obsessed with 'the possibility that women might have sexual desires that were independent of their role as passive receptacles of male desire'.

That Hellena in *The Rover* falls in love with Willmore for all the wrong reasons may tell us more about Aphra Behn's own unfortunate liaisons than about Hellena: but neither the character nor her creator was a 'passive receptacle'. What Behn did achieve, in her writing if not perhaps in her life, was a triumphant assertion of women's rights to their own sexuality, and at least the tentative expression – if her plays were to remain commercial, it could be no more than tentative – of her belief that true sexual satisfaction for both men *and* women lay in close and reciprocal relationships, not in the yoking of sexuality to property rights and family trees.

'The Injuries of Age and Time'

For a woman whose plays make what appear to us quite proper claims for the independence of her sex, Aphra Behn numbered among her closest acquaintances many men – apart from the king himself, the likes of Sedley, Buckingham, and Rochester – who were liberated in their own sexuality, but unenlightened in their attitudes towards women. Rochester, like most of these courtly wits, was no 'mere' rake. Though credited with training one of his mistresses, Elizabeth Barry, for the stage, he undertook the exercise less from interest in her own non-sexual attributes than to win a bet with his male companions. Behn was indebted to Rochester as a patron, but appears genuinely to have liked and admired the man, with whom she exchanged bawdy poems. A chronic drunkard as well as a poet, a ravisher of pretty women and a fancier of young boys, Rochester, who is often named as the model for the fashionable wit Dorimant in Etherege's *The Man of Mode,* was capable of scandalising even the king's sense of decency with some of his more public outrages.

Rochester may well have been on Aphra Behn's mind when she tried to make Willmore in *The Rover* so sexually magnetic. But there were others in Behn's circle with a claim to be the model for such a character. There was John Greenhill, the highly talented portrait painter, who, like Rochester, died probably of syphilis in his early thirties. Aphra Behn wrote an elegy to his memory and sent a copy to Rochester: he had at least been spared 'the injuries of age and time'. In lighter-hearted vein, she made poetic mock of another male acquaintance for his misfortune in contracting syphilis – not an uncommon ailment in her circle, and one from which she was possibly herself a sufferer in later years. If so, she probably picked up the disease during the longest and stormiest of her own love affairs, with the bisexual rake, lawyer, man of letters, and chief claimant to be the original of Willmore – John Hoyle.

Suspected of the republican sympathies which had led his father to take his own life, Hoyle was in other respects entirely a man of the Restoration. He was attractive to women, and appears to have treated all his conquests with the amused contempt which so exasperated Aphra Behn. Her poems suggest that, despite her own previous liaisons, this affair – which would have been at its tempestuous height around the time she was writing *The Rover* – was the one in which she felt the most complete consummation of her sexual passion. Yet Hoyle kept Behn, like all his mistresses, at a distance, pursuing his other affairs while wishing her to remain faithful to him alone; inflicting casual insults upon her, yet highly sensitive to any imagined slights in her own behaviour.

Aphra Behn's remaining letters to Hoyle seem to be half-persuading, half-pleading for the kind of freedom, combined with commitment of the heart, to which Hellena in *The Rover* believes she had led Willmore. But Behn's biographer Angeline Goreau suggests that part of Hoyle's attraction was precisely the knowledge that she would never be called upon to act out the role of wife for him, any more than that of conventional mistress. She suffered, but she kept her freedom. So, presumably, did her Hellena – who conspicuously fails to appear in the undistinguished sequel to *The Rover*, *The Second Part of The Rover* (1680), in which Willmore has conveniently become a widower.

The death of Charles II in 1685 marked the close of an era that was already turning sour. John Hoyle was tried incon-clusively for sodomy in 1687, by which time the affair with Behn was probably over. He outlived her only by three years, before being killed in a tavern brawl – for which his murderer successfully pleaded self-defence. Greenhill and Rochester were already dead, burned out by debauchery, and Buckingham was not only out of favour politically but 'worn to a thread with whoring'. Among Aphra Behn's playwriting friends, Wycherley was in a debtors' prison, Nathaniel Lee was on public exhibition in a madhouse, and Otway was starving to death in a slum – despite, it seems, some financial help from Behn, although she was herself in debt. She died – some said of a minor ailment ineptly treated – with a fine sense of timing, a few days after the coronation of William and Mary, whose accession ended the era with whose values Aphra Behn was so closely identified. *The Rover*, written in 1677, just a year before the 'Popish Plot', may in retrospect be seen as one of the last celebrations of the Restoration spirit, in which no real sense of doubt or danger lurks in the darker corners of bedchamber or tavern.

'The Rover' as Restoration Comedy

Critics of Aphra Behn's play find themselves in a paradoxical position. The works are inseparably linked with those social and political conditions which I have tried to outline in earlier sections, as they are also with their author's personal feelings about those conditions. Yet we know so few details of Behn's life, outside her purely professional activities, that any conjectural reconstruction inevitably leads us . . . back full circle to the plays themselves.

Perhaps the chief gain from getting caught up in this critical double-bind is the way in which characters in Behn's plays – which one would otherwise tend to categorise as 'types' – come to take on ampler dimensions. Fluent gallants have been sparring in verbal duels with their pert mistresses in a literary lineage which stretches from Shakespeare's Beatrice and Benedick to Congreve's Mirabell and Millamant and beyond – for example, to Bernard Shaw's Jack Tanner and Ann Whitefield in *Man and Superman*. And critics have conventionally 'placed' such couples with references to the 'enduring' psychological interest of love-hate relationships, or the downright metaphysical workings of the life-force, rather than to the social contexts within which such sexual masquerades were conducted. But the duels of wit in *The Rover* – as in the other examples cited, for that matter – are fought within a complex web of sexual, social and economic prejudices inseparable from their time.

Or, to take a different tangent: the character regarded by most critics, even the most sympathetic, as an unsatisfactory loose-end to the plot, Angellica Bianca (though sharing her initials as well as her temperament with her creator), becomes nothing so simple as an authorial mouthpiece, or as theatrically irrelevant as a self-portrait, but a 'loose-end' left over by society itself. Angellica is the sexually attractive woman who has rejected the loss of independence involved in marriage: she has therefore exploited her only form of inherited 'capital' – her looks – in part as revenge against the male sex, which has reduced her to that expedient. But the repudiation by Willmore represents for her not just the scorning of real love painfully exposed, but a first reminder that loss of beauty will leave her with a future of economic uncertainty as well as personal loneliness.

When the critic L.C. Knights launched his influential attack on Restoration comedy just before the Second World War, he was using the term in its commonly vague sense, to embrace the work of Congreve, Vanbrugh, and even Farquhar – all of whom wrote long after the values of the 'chronological' Restoration had been extinguished, and who were all too conscious of the moral critique of their work initiated in 1698 by Jeremy Collier. A century or so later, all that an apologetic Charles Lamb could suggest by way of excuse for these dissolute comedies was that they were 'artificial' – set in a 'Utopia of gallantry' with 'no reference whatsoever to the world that is'. Whether or not that is true of the later plays of Congreve and Vanbrugh, Aphra Behn helps us to view the actual world of the Restoration from a new angle which also gives added depth to the work of her closer contemporaries, Etherege, Otway, and Wycherley, and confirms that all are writing about a very 'real' if limited range of experience.

The Rover, of course, is unusual in that it is not set in the fashionable West End drawing-rooms and walks of Restoration London, but in a recent past to which a due proportion of its audiences in 1677 probably looked back a mite nostalgically (just as

Londoners often looked back fondly to the camaraderie of the Blitz, despite its dangers and deprivations). True, this is still the world of 'the town', and the rustic simpleton Ned Blunt can expect to fall into its snares as surely as he would have done in London: but the advantage of 'foreignness' also means that Belvile and his companions are less sure-footed socially, just as they are free of the constraints of class expectations or family ties. In such freedoms from traditional constraints the 'actual' Restoration sensibility also had its roots.

And so, perhaps a trifle schematically, Aphra Behn shows her exiles spanning a whole spectrum of attitudes to women and to love – from the mere loutishness of Blunt, through the butterfly charm of Willmore and the almost accidental amours of Frederick, to the romantic single-heartedness of Belvile. Each has his theatrical ancestors, but each is also part of an historical moment. Each meets his match, and gets his sexual if not his moral desserts.

All moral judgements are relative. When Gilbert Burnet cautioned Rochester against womanising, his ostensibly Christian grounds of reproof were that it was wrong to rob a father or a husband of their property. When Hellena casts off her gypsy disguise and reveals that she has a fortune at her disposal, the only choice she has in deciding its and her own fate is between a nunnery and marriage. In declaring for Willmore, she is 'disposing' of her fortune indeed. It *should* not have been so, of course: but precisely because Behn's characters are not living in an 'artificial' world divorced from the social *mores* of their time, it would have been pointless for her to attempt any more 'morally appropriate' conclusion. The only alternative is the angry independence enjoyed by Angellica, and Aphra Behn does not attempt to suggest a conclusion to that.

Many of those parents who preferred to trust their own financial acumen rather than their daughter's emotional inclinations in choosing her a husband sincerely believed that lasting security was more important to a woman than perhaps fleeting sexual fulfilment. Restoration comedy occasionally twisted the rules of the game by allowing the two to coincide – but it also accepted that 'rules' which did not generally relate love to marriage therefore permitted love outside marriage. The alleged hypocrisy of such plays is arguably the reverse – an openness, confessedly uncritical, about a state of sexual affairs which continued well into the Victorian era, although by that time openness had been overlain with hypocrisy.

Our own century's confused response to Restoration comedy suggests that it continues to touch us near the quick. It was only permissible as a kind of make-believe once the Romantics had idealised sexual relationships without altering their economic base, but it came into a somewhat prettified version of its own during the nineteen twenties, when a fresh wave of the sexual revolution broke – but again touched only the upper classes. Once the 'bright young things' of the 'twenties were swept away, Restoration comedy suffered stern critical rebuffs in the self-improving 'forties, until the 'permissive society' seemed to be spreading a gospel of sexual openness to all sections of society. Now, productions veer between those striving to uncover the social realities beneath the conventions, and those which take the plays out of time altogether. But none can ignore, even if they seek to avoid, what emerging feminist consciousness taught us in the nineteen seventies – that 'sexual openness' no more signified equality then than it had done three hundred years earlier.

As a feminist in her own time, that is one of the things that Aphra Behn had been saying all along. As a professional playwright with no alternative source of income, she could not, however, say it very loudly. That was *her* critical double-bind.

For Further Reading

There are useful scholarly editions of *The Rover* edited by
Frederick M. Link in the Regents Restoration Drama Series
(London, 1967), and by Marion Lomax in the New Mermaids
series (London, 1995). Selections of Aphra Behn's plays include
Five Plays, introduced by Maureen Duffy (London, 1990) and *The
Rover and Other Plays*, edited by Jane Spencer (Oxford, 1995). Janet
Todd's Penguin selection (London, 1992) also includes Behn's
novel, *Oroonoko*. The first volume of Todd's six-volume *The Works
of Aphra Behn* (London, 1992–95) contains a valuable introduction.

Of the major modern biographies of Behn, Maureen Duffy's *The
Passionate Shepherdess: Aphra Behn* (London, 1977) is the more
pertinently critical about the works themselves, while Angeline
Goreau's *Reconstructing Aphra* (Oxford, 1980) is the more helpful on
the socio-political context. Frederick M. Link's *Behn* (New York,
1968) was the first full-length critical study. All three of these
include extensive bibliographies of work on Behn before the
upsurge in feminist interest from the 'eighties onwards. This is
exemplified by Aphra Behn's inclusion in Sara Heller
Mendelson's *The Mental World of Stuart Women* (Brighton, 1987),
though Jacqueline Pearson's *The Prostituted Muse: Images of Women
and Women Dramatists 1642–1737* (Brighton, 1988) is more
specifically dramatic in orientation. A selection of other recent
writings on her work, *Rereading Aphra Behn: History, Theory and
Criticism*, has been edited by Heidi Hutner (Charlottesville, 1993).

Of the many general studies of Restoration theatre, the
introduction to the definitive but massive 'calendar', *The London
Stage*, has usefully been reprinted as a separate volume, *The London*

Stage 1660–1700: a Critical Introduction, by Emmett L. Avery and
Arthur H. Scouten (Carbondale, 1968), while the fifth volume of
The Revels History of Drama in English, covering the period 1660 to
1750, edited by John Loftis and others (London, 1976), usefully
blends theatre history with dramatic criticism. Robert D. Hume's
The Development of English Drama in the Late Seventeenth Century
(Oxford, 1976) offers fuller coverage of Behn's work in its context,
though is less theatrically oriented than Jocelyn Powell's *Restoration
Theatre Practice* (London, 1984) or Peter Holland's *The Ornament of
Action* (Cambridge, 1979), both of which are valuable on stage
practice – but, like so much writing on Restoration theatre until
the late 'eighties, neglectful of Behn's own works.

Aphra Behn: Key Dates

1640   *c.* Born, conjecturally in early July, at Wye or Sturry, near Canterbury, Kent. Maiden name Amies, Johnson, or Cooper.

1663   *c.* Family in Surinam, but her father, who had been appointed Lieutenant-General, died on the voyage. Stayed on a local plantation.

1664   Returned to London in the spring. Presented an Indian costume to the King's Company.

1665   *c.* Marriage to Mr. Behn, probably a Dutch merchant, who died soon afterwards.

1666   Persuaded by Thomas Killigrew to serve as a spy in the Dutch Wars, but discovered little of value while in Antwerp, and remained unpaid for her services.

1667   Returned to London.

1668   Committed to prison for debt, despite petitions to Killigrew and the King. Date of release uncertain.

1670   December, her first play, the tragi-comic *The Forced Marriage*, performed by the Duke's Company at Lincoln's Inn Fields, achieving a run of six nights. Around this time, beginning of her long relationship with the dissolute lawyer John Hoyle.

1671   Her second tragi-comedy, *The Amorous Prince*, at Lincoln's Inn Fields in the spring.

1673   February, failure of her comedy of intrigue *The Dutch Lover* at Dorset Garden.

1676   The passionate tragedy *Abdelazer* performed at Dorset Garden in July, followed there in September by a 'scandalous' comedy with brothel scenes, *The Town Fop*.

1677   March, *The Rover* produced at Dorset Garden. Two other plays attributed to her also seen at Dorset Garden, *The Debauchee* in February and *The Counterfeit Bridegroom* in September.

1678   January, *Sir Patient Fancy,* a comedy adapted from Molière's *The Imaginary Invalid,* at Dorset Garden.

1679   Beginning of the exclusion crisis. The comedy *The Feigned Courtesans* at Dorset Garden in the spring, and the tragi-comedy *The Young King* in early autumn.

1681   April, *The Second Part of The Rover;* November, the farcical comedy *The False Count;* and December, the historical comedy *The Roundheads:* all at Dorset Garden.

1682   The anti-Whig political lampoon *The City Heiress* 'well received' at Dorset Garden in the spring, but *Like Father, Like Son* which failed there, remained unprinted. Increasing hostility from the Whigs leads to her arrest for the prologue she contributed in August to the anonymous *Romulus and Hersilia.* She largely abandons writing for the theatre. Merging of the two companies.

1683   Wrote three of her posthumously published short novels.

1684   Published her *Poems on Several Occasions.*

1685   Publication of her poetic *Miscellany.* Death of Charles II and accession of his brother James II.

1686   The prose work *La Montre; or, The Lover's Watch* published. Returned to the theatre in April with the comedy *The Lucky Chance* at Drury Lane.

1687   *The Emperor of the Moon,* one of her greatest successes, first seen at Drury Lane in March.

1688   Published the short novels *The Fair Jilt, Agnes de Castro,* and *Oroonoko.* The 'bloodless revolution' establishes the protestant supremacy under William and Mary.

1689   16 April, died, and buried in Westminster Abbey. Posthumous production in November of her last play, the comedy *The Widow Ranter,* at Drury Lane, a failure. The comedy *The Younger Brother* also first produced posthumously, at Drury Lane in February 1696.

THE ROVER

Prologue

Written by a person of quality

Wits, like physicians, never can agree,
When of a different society.
And Rabel's drops were never more cried down
By all the learned doctors of the town,
Than a new play, whose author is unknown:
Nor can those doctors with more malice sue
(And powerful purses) the dissenting few
Than those with an insulting pride do rail
At all who are not of their own cabal.

If a young poet hit your humour right,
You judge him then out of revenge and spite;
So amongst men there are ridiculous elves,
Who monkeys hate for being too like themselves.
So that the reason of the grand debate,
Why wit so oft is damned, when good plays take,
Is that you censure as you love or hate.

Thus like a learned conclave poets sit,
Catholic judges both of sense and wit,
And damn or save, as they themselves think fit.
Yet those who to others' faults are so severe,
Are not so perfect, but themselves may err.
Some write correct indeed, but then the whole
(Bating their own dull stuff i' th' play) is stole:
As bees do suck from flowers their honey-dew,
So they rob others, striving to please you.

Some write their characters genteel and fine,
But then they do so toil for every line
That what to you does easy seem, and plain,
Is the hard issue of their labouring brain.
And some th' effects of all their pains we see,
Is but to mimic good extempore.
Others, by long converse about the town,
Have wit enough to write a lewd lampoon,
But their chief skill lies in a bawdy song.
In short, the only wit that's now in fashion
Is but the gleanings of good conversation.
As for the author of this coming play,
I asked him what he thought fit I should say,
In thanks for your good company today:
He called me fool, and said it was well known,
You came not here for our sakes, but your own.
New plays are stuffed with wits, and with debauches,
That crowd and sweat like cits in May Day coaches.

4

The Persons of the Play

MEN
DON ANTONIO, *the Viceroy's son*
DON PEDRO, *a noble Spaniard, his friend*
BELVILE, *an English Colonel in love with Florinda*
WILLMORE, *the Rover*
FREDERICK, *an English gentleman, and friend to Belvile and Blunt*
BLUNT, *an English country gentleman*
STEPHANO, *servant to Don Pedro*
PHILIPPO, *Lucetta's gallant*
SANCHO, *pimp to Lucetta*
BISKEY *and* SEBASTIAN, *two bravos to Angellica*
DIEGO, *page to Don Antonio*
PAGE *to Hellena*
BOY, *page to Belvile*
BLUNT'S MAN
OFFICERS, SOLDIERS, MASQUERADERS (*men and women*)

WOMEN
FLORINDA, *sister to Don Pedro*
HELLENA, *a gay young woman, designed for a nun, sister to Florinda*
VALERIA, *a kinswoman to Florinda*
ANGELLICA BIANCA, *a famous courtesan*
MORETTA, *her woman*
CALLIS, *governess to Florinda and Hellena*
LUCETTA, *a jilting wench*

Scene: Naples, in carnival time.

Act I, Scene i

A chamber. Enter FLORINDA *and* HELLENA.

FLORINDA. What an impertinent thing is a young girl bred in a nunnery! How full of questions! Prithee no more, Hellena; I have told thee more than thou understand'st already.

HELLENA. The more's my grief; I would fain know as much as you, which makes me so inquisitive; nor is't enough I know you're a lover, unless you tell me too, who 'tis you sigh for.

FLORINDA. When you're a lover, I'll think you fit for a secret of that nature.

HELLENA. 'Tis true, I never was a lover yet – but I begin to have a shrewd guess, what 'tis to be so, and fancy it very pretty to sigh, and sing, and blush and wish, and dream and wish, and long and wish to see the man; and when I do, look pale and tremble, just as you did when my brother brought home the fine English Colonel to see you – what do you call him, Don Belvile?

FLORINDA. Fie, Hellena.

HELLENA. That blush betrays you – I am sure 'tis so – or is it Don Antonio the viceroy's son? – or perhaps the rich old Don Vincentio, whom my father designs you for a husband? – Why do you blush again?

FLORINDA. With indignation; and how near soever my father thinks I am to marrying that hated object, I shall let him see I understand better what's due to my beauty, birth, and fortune, and more to my soul, than to obey those unjust commands.

HELLENA. Now hang me if I don't love thee for that dear disobedience. I love mischief strangely, as most of our sex do, who are come to love nothing else – but tell me, dear Florinda, don't you love that fine *Anglese?* For I vow, next to loving him myself, 'twill please me most that you do so, for he is so gay and so handsome.

FLORINDA. Hellena, a maid designed for a nun ought not to be so curious in a discourse of love.

HELLENA. And dost thou think that ever I'll be a nun? Or at least till I'm so old, I'm fit for nothing else. Faith, no, sister; and that which makes me long to know whether you love Belvile, is because I hope he has some mad companion or other, that will spoil my devotion. Nay, I'm resolved to provide myself this carnival, if there be e'er a handsome proper fellow of my humour above ground, though I ask first.

FLORINDA. Prithee be not so wild.

HELLENA. Now you have provided yourself of a man, you take no care for poor me. Prithee tell me, what dost thou see about me that is unfit for love? Have I not a world of youth? A humour gay? A beauty passable? A vigour desirable? Well shaped? Clean limbed? Sweet breathed? And sense enough to know how all these ought to be employed to the best advantage? Yes, I do and will. Therefore lay aside your hopes of my fortune, by my being a devotee, and tell me how you came acquainted with this Belvile; for I perceive you knew him before he came to Naples.

FLORINDA. Yes, I knew him at the siege of Pamplona: he was then a colonel of French horse, who when the town was ransacked, nobly treated my brother and myself, preserving us from all insolences; and I must own (besides great obligations) I have I know not what, that pleads kindly for him about my heart, and will suffer no other to enter. – But see, my brother.

Enter DON PEDRO, STEPHANO, *with a masquing habit, and* CALLIS.

PEDRO. Good morrow, sister. Pray, when saw you your lover Don Vincentio?

FLORINDA. I know not, sir. – Callis, when was he here? For I consider it so little, I know not when it was.

PEDRO. I have a command from my father here to tell you, you ought not to despise him, a man of so vast a fortune, and such a passion for you. – Stephano, my things.

Puts on his masquing habit.

FLORINDA. A passion for me! 'Tis more than e'er I saw, or he had a desire should be known. I hate Vincentio, sir, and I would not have a man so dear to me as my brother follow the ill customs of our country, and make a slave of his sister. – And sir, my father's will, I'm sure, you may divert.

PEDRO. I know not how dear I am to you, but I wish only to be ranked in your esteem, equal with the English Colonel Belvile. – Why do you frown and blush? Is there any guilt belongs to the name of that cavalier?

FLORINDA. I'll not deny I value Belvile: when I was exposed to such dangers as the licensed lust of common soldiers threatened, when rage and conquest flew through the city – then Belvile, this criminal for my sake, threw himself into all dangers to save my honour; and will you not allow him my esteem?

PEDRO. Yes, pay him what you will in honour – but you must consider Don Vincentio's fortune, and the jointure he'll make you.

FLORINDA. Let him consider my youth, beauty and fortune; which ought not to be thrown away on his age and jointure.

PEDRO. 'Tis true, he's not so young and fine a gentleman as that Belvile – but what jewels will that cavalier present you with? Those of his eyes and heart?

HELLENA. And are not those better than any Don Vincentio has brought from the Indies?

PEDRO. Why how now! Has your nunnery-breeding taught you to understand the value of hearts and eyes?

HELLENA. Better than to believe Vincentio's deserve value from any woman. He may perhaps increase her bags, but not her family.

PEDRO. This is fine – go up to your devotion, you are not designed for the conversation of lovers.

HELLENA (*aside*). Nor saints, yet awhile, I hope. [*To* PEDRO.] – Is't not enough you make a nun of me, but you must cast my sister away too, exposing her to a worse confinement than a religious life?

PEDRO. The girl's mad. Is it a confinement to be carried into the country, to an ancient villa belonging to the family of the Vincentios these five hundred years, and have no other prospect than that pleasing one of seeing all her own that meets her eyes – a fine air, large fields and gardens, where she may walk and gather flowers?

HELLENA. When? By moon-light? For I am sure she dares not encounter with the heat of the sun; that were a task only for Don Vincentio and his Indian breeding, who loves it in the dog-days. – And if these be her daily divertissements, what are those of the night? To lie in a wide moth-eaten bed-chamber with furniture in fashion in the reign of King Sancho the First; the bed, that which his forefathers lived and died in.

PEDRO. Very well.

HELLENA. This apartment (new furbished and fitted out for the young wife) he (out of freedom) makes his dressing room;

and being a frugal and a jealous coxcomb, instead of a valet to uncase his feeble carcass, he desires you to do that office – signs of favour, I'll assure you, and such as you must not hope for, unless your woman be out of the way.

PEDRO. Have you done yet?

HELLENA. That honour being past, the giant stretches himself, yawns and sighs a belch or two, loud as a musket, throws himself into bed, and expects you in his foul sheets, and e'er you can get yourself undressed, calls you with a snore or two. – And are not these fine blessings to a young lady?

PEDRO. Have you done yet?

HELLENA. And this man you must kiss, nay, you must kiss none but him too – and nuzzle through his beard to find his lips – and this you must submit to for threescore years, and all for a jointure.

PEDRO. For all your character of Don Vincentio, she is as like to marry him as she was before.

HELLENA. Marry Don Vincentio! Hang me, such a wedlock would be worse than adultery with another man. I had rather see her in the *Hostel de Dieu*, to waste her youth there in vows and be a handmaid to lazars and cripples, than to lose it in such a marriage.

PEDRO. You have considered, sister, that Belvile has no fortune to bring to you, banished his country, despised at home, and pitied abroad?

HELLENA. What then? The Viceroy's son is better than that old Sir Fisty. Don Vincentio! Don Indian! He thinks he's trading to Gambo still, and would barter himself (that bell and bauble) for your youth and fortune.

PEDRO. Callis, take her hence, and lock her up all this carnival, and at Lent she shall begin her everlasting penance in a monastery.

HELLENA. I care not. I had rather be a nun, than be obliged to marry as you would have me, if I were designed for't.

PEDRO. Do not fear the blessing of that choice – you shall be a nun.

HELLENA (*aside*). Shall I so? You may chance to be mistaken in my way of devotion – a nun! Yes, I am like to make a fine nun! I have an excellent humour for a grate. No, I'll have a saint of my own to pray to shortly, if I like any that dares venture on me.

PEDRO. Callis, make it your business to watch this wild cat. As for you, Florinda, I've only tried you all this while, and urged my father's will; but mine is, that you would love Antonio, he is brave and young, and all that can complete the happiness of a gallant maid. – This absence of my father will give us opportunity to free you from Vincentio, by marrying here, which you must do tomorrow.

FLORINDA. Tomorrow!

PEDRO. Tomorrow, or 'twill be too late – 'tis not my friendship to Antonio which makes me urge this, but love to thee and hatred to Vincentio – therefore resolve upon tomorrow.

FLORINDA. Sir, I shall strive to do, as shall become your sister.

PEDRO. I'll both believe and trust you – adieu.

Exeunt PEDRO *and* STEPHANO.

HELLENA. As becomes his sister! That is to be as resolved your way, as he is his.

HELLENA *goes to* CALLIS.

FLORINDA. I ne'er till now perceived my ruin near,
I've no defence against Antonio's love,
For he has all the advantages of nature,
The moving arguments of youth and fortune.

HELLENA. But hark you, Callis, you will not be so cruel to lock me up indeed: will you?

CALLIS. I must obey the commands I hate – besides, do you consider what a life you are going to lead?

HELLENA. Yes, Callis, that of a nun: and till then I'll be indebted a world of prayers to you, if you'll let me now see, what I never did, the divertissements of a carnival.

CALLIS. What, go in masquerade? 'Twill be a fine farewell to the world, I take it — pray what would you do there?

HELLENA. That which all the world does, as I am told – be as mad as the rest, and take all innocent freedoms. – Sister, you'll go too, will you not? Come prithee be not sad – we'll outwit twenty brothers, if you'll be ruled by me. – Come put off this dull humour with your clothes, and assume one as gay, and as fantastic as the dress my cousin Valeria and I have provided, and let's ramble.

FLORINDA. Callis, will you give us leave to go?

CALLIS (*aside*). I have a youthful itch of going myself. [*To* FLORINDA.] – Madam, if I thought your brother might not know it, and I might wait on you; for by my troth I'll not trust young girls alone.

FLORINDA. Thou see'st my brother's gone already, and thou shalt attend and watch us.

Enter STEPHANO.

STEPHANO. Madam, the habits are come, and your cousin Valeria is dressed, and stays for you.

FLORINDA. 'Tis well – I'll write a note, and if I chance to see Belvile, and want an opportunity to speak to him, that shall let him know what I've resolved in favour of him.

HELLENA. Come, let's in and dress us.

Exeunt.

Act I, Scene ii

A long street. Enter BELVILE, *melancholy,* BLUNT *and* FREDERICK.

FREDERICK. Why, what the devil ails the Colonel, in a time when all the world is gay, to look like mere Lent thus? Hadst thou been long enough in Naples to have been in love, I should have sworn some such judgement had befallen thee.

BELVILE. No, I have made no new amours since I came to Naples.

FREDERICK. You have left none behind you in Paris?

BELVILE. Neither.

FREDERICK. I cannot divine the cause then; unless the old cause, the want of money.

BLUNT. And another old cause, the want of a wench – would not that revive you?

BELVILE. You are mistaken, Ned.

BLUNT. Nay, 'sheartlikins, then thou'rt past cure.

FREDERICK. I have found it out; thou hast renewed thy acquaintance with the lady that cost thee so many sighs at the siege of Pamplona – pox on't, what d'ye call her – her brother's a noble Spaniard – nephew to the dead general – Florinda – ay, Florinda – and will nothing serve thy turn but that damned virtuous woman, whom on my conscience thou lov'st in spite too, because thou seest little or no possibility of gaining her?

BELVILE. Thou art mistaken; I have int'rest enough in that lovely virgin's heart to make me proud and vain, were it not abated by the severity of her brother Pedro, who perceiving my happiness –

FREDERICK. Has civilly forbid thee the house?

BELVILE. 'Tis so, to make way for a powerful rival, the Viceroy's son, who has the advantage of me in being a man of fortune, a Spaniard, and her brother's friend; which gives him liberty to make his court, whilst I have recourse only to letters, and distant looks from her window, which are as soft and kind as those which Heaven sends down on penitents.

BLUNT. Hey day! 'Sheartlikins, simile! By this light the man is quite spoiled.

FREDERICK. What the devil are we made of, that we cannot be thus concerned for a wench?

BLUNT. 'Sheartlikins, our Cupids are like the cooks of the camp – they can roast or boil a woman, but they have none of the fine tricks to set 'em off, no hogoes to make the sauce pleasant, and the stomach sharp.

FREDERICK. I dare swear I have had a hundred as young, kind and handsome as this Florinda; and dogs eat me, if they were not as troublesome to me i' th' morning as they were welcome o'er night.

BLUNT. And yet, I warrant, he would not touch another woman, if he might have her for nothing.

BELVILE. That's thy joy, a cheap whore.

BLUNT. Why, 'sheartlikins, I love a frank soul. – When did you ever hear of an honest woman that took a man's money? I warrant 'em good ones. – But gentlemen, you may be free; you have been kept so poor with parliaments and protectors, that the little stock you have is not worth preserving – but I thank my stars, I had more grace than to forfeit my estate by cavaliering.

BELVILE. Methinks only following the court should be sufficient to entitle 'em to that.

BLUNT. 'Sheartlikins, they know I follow it to do it no good, unless they pick a hole in my coat for lending you money now and then; which is a greater crime to my conscience, gentlemen, than to the Commonwealth.

Enter WILLMORE.

WILLMORE. Ha! Dear Belvile! Noble colonel!

BELVILE. Willmore! Welcome ashore, my dear rover! – What happy wind blew us this good fortune?

WILLMORE. Let me salute my dear Fred, and then command me. – How is't, honest lad?

FREDERICK. Faith, sir, the old compliment, infinitely the better to see my dear mad Willmore again. – Prithee why camest thou ashore? And where's the Prince?

WILLMORE. He's well, and reigns still lord of the watery element. – I must aboard again within a day or two, and my business ashore was only to enjoy myself a little this carnival.

BELVILE. Pray know our new friend, sir; he's but bashful, a raw traveller, but honest, stout, and one of us.

Embraces BLUNT.

WILLMORE. That you esteem him, gives him an int'rest here.

BLUNT. Your servant, sir.

WILLMORE. But well, faith, I'm glad to meet you again in a warm climate, where the kind sun has its god-like power still over the wine and women. – Love and mirth are my business in Naples; and if I mistake not the place, here's an excellent market for chapmen of my humour.

BELVILE. See, here be those kind merchants of love you look for.

Enter several MEN *in masquing habits, some playing on musical instruments, others dancing after;* WOMEN *dressed like courtesans, with papers pinned on their breasts, and baskets of flowers in their hands.*

BLUNT. 'Sheartlikins, what have we here!

FREDERICK. Now the game begins.

WILLMORE. Fine pretty creatures! May a stranger have leave to look and love? – What's here? (*Reads the papers.*) – 'Roses for every month!'

BLUNT. Roses for every month! What means that?

BELVILE. They are, or would have you think they're courtesans, who here in Naples are to be hired by the month.

WILLMORE. Kind and obliging to inform us. – [*To a* WOMAN.] Pray where do these roses grow? I would fain plant some of 'em in a bed of mine.

WOMAN. Beware such roses, sir.

WILLMORE. A pox of fear: I'll be baked with thee between a pair of sheets, and that's thy proper still; so I might but strew such roses over me and under me. – Fair one, would you would give me leave to gather at your bush this idle month, I would go near to make somebody smell of it all the year after.

BELVILE. And thou hast need of such a remedy, for thou stink'st of tar and ropes' ends, like a dock or pest-house.

The WOMAN *puts herself into the hands of a* MAN *and exit.*

WILLMORE. Nay, nay, you shall not leave me so.

BELVILE. By all means use no violence here.

WILLMORE. Death! Just as I was going to be damnably in love, to have her led off! I could pluck that rose out of his hand, and even kiss the bed, the bush grew in.

FREDERICK. No friend to love like a long voyage at sea.

BLUNT. Except a nunnery, Fred.

WILLMORE. Death! But will they not be kind, quickly be kind? Thou know'st I'm no tame sigher, but a rampant lion of the forest.

Advances, from the farther end of the scenes, two men dressed all over with horns of several sorts, making grimaces at one another, with papers pinned on their backs.

BELVILE. Oh the fantastical rogues, how they're dressed! 'Tis a satire against the whole sex.

WILLMORE. Is this a fruit that grows in this warm country?

BELVILE. Yes: 'tis pretty to see these Italians start, swell, and stab at the word cuckold, and yet stumble at horns on every threshold.

WILLMORE. See what's on their back. (*Reads.*) 'Flowers of every night.' – Ah rogue! And more sweet than roses of ev'ry month! This is a gardener of Adam's own breeding.

They dance.

BELVILE. What think you of those grave people? – Is a wake in Essex half so mad or extravagant?

WILLMORE. I like their sober grave way, 'tis a kind of legal authorised fornication, where the men are not chid for't, nor the women despised, as amongst our dull English. Even the monsieurs want that part of good manners.

BELVILE. But here in Italy, a monsieur is the humblest best-bred gentleman. – Duels are so baffled by bravos that an age shows not one, but between a Frenchman and a hang-man, who is as much too hard for him on the Piazza, as they are for a Dutchman on the New Bridge. – But see, another crew.

Enter FLORINDA, HELLENA, *and* VALERIA, *dressed like gipsies;* CALLIS *and* STEPHANO, LUCETTA, PHILIPPO *and* SANCHO *in masquerade.*

HELLENA. Sister, there's your Englishman, and with him a handsome proper fellow. I'll to him, and instead of telling him his fortune, try my own.

WILLMORE. Gipsies, on my life. – Sure these will prattle if a man cross their hands. (*Goes to* HELLENA.) – Dear, pretty (and I hope) young devil, will you tell an amorous stranger what luck he's like to have?

HELLENA. Have a care how you venture with me, sir, lest I pick your pocket, which will more vex your English humour, than an Italian fortune will please you.

WILLMORE. How the devil cam'st thou to know my country and humour?

HELLENA. The first I guess by a certain forward impudence, which does not displease me at this time; and the loss of your money will vex you, because I hope you have but very little to lose.

WILLMORE. Egad, child, thou'rt i' th' right; it is so little I dare not offer it thee for a kindness. – But cannot you divine what other things of more value I have about me, that I would more willingly part with?

HELLENA. Indeed no, that's the business of a witch, and I am but a gipsy yet. – Yet without looking in your hand, I have a parlous guess, 'tis some foolish heart you mean, an inconstant English heart, as little worth stealing as your purse.

WILLMORE. Nay, then thou dost deal with the devil, that's certain. – Thou hast guessed as right as if thou hadst been one of that number it has languished for. I find you'll be better acquainted with it; nor can you take it in a better time, for I am come from sea, child; and Venus not being propitious to me in her own element, I have a world of love in store. – Would you would be good-natured and take some on't off my hands.

HELLENA. Why – I could be inclined that way – but for a
   foolish vow I am going to make – to die a maid.

WILLMORE. Then thou art damned without redemption; and
   as I am a good Christian, I ought in charity to divert so
   wicked a design; therefore prithee, dear creature, let me
   know quickly when and where I shall begin to set a helping
   hand to so good a work.

HELLENA. If you should prevail with my tender heart (as
   I begin to fear you will, for you have horrible loving eyes)
   there will be difficulty in't, that you'll hardly undergo for
   my sake.

WILLMORE. Faith, child, I have been bred in dangers, and wear
   a sword that has been employed in a worse cause than for a
   handsome kind woman. – Name the danger – let it be any
   thing but a long siege, and I'll undertake it.

HELLENA. Can you storm?

WILLMORE. Oh, most furiously.

HELLENA. What think you of a nunnery wall? For he that wins
   me must gain that first.

WILLMORE. A nun! Oh, how I love thee for't! There's no
   sinner like a young saint. – Nay, now there's no denying me;
   the old law had no curse (to a woman) like dying a maid:
   witness Jephthah's daughter.

HELLENA. A very good text this, if well handled; and I perceive, Father Captain, you would impose no severe penance
   on her who were inclined to console herself before she took
   orders.

WILLMORE. If she be young and handsome.

HELLENA. Ay, there's it – but if she be not –

WILLMORE. By this hand, child, I have an implicit faith, and
   dare venture on thee with all faults. – Besides, 'tis more

meritorious to leave the world when thou hast tasted and proved the pleasure on't; then 'twill be a virtue in thee, which now will be pure ignorance.

HELLENA. I perceive, good Father Captain, you design only to make me fit for Heaven – but if on the contrary you should quite divert me from it, and bring me back to the world again, I should have a new man to seek, I find; and what a grief that will be – for when I begin, I fancy I shall love like anything: I never tried yet.

WILLMORE. Egad, and that's kind. – Prithee, dear creature, give me credit for a heart, for faith, I'm a very honest fellow. – Oh, I long to come first to the banquet of love; and such a swinging appetite I bring. Oh, I'm impatient. Thy lodging, sweetheart, thy lodging, or I'm a dead man.

HELLENA. Why must we be either guilty of fornication or murder if we converse with you men? – And is there no difference between leave to love me, and leave to lie with me?

WILLMORE. Faith, child, they were made to go together.

LUCETTA (*pointing to* BLUNT). Are you sure this is the man?

They withdraw.

SANCHO. When did I mistake your game?

LUCETTA. This is a stranger, I know by his gazing; if he be brisk he'll venture to follow me; and then, if I understand my trade, he's mine. He's English too, and they say that's a sort of good-natured loving people, and have generally so kind an opinion of themselves, that a woman with any wit may flatter 'em into any sort of fool she pleases.

She often passes by BLUNT *and gazes on him; he struts, and cocks, and walks, and gazes on her.*

BLUNT. 'Tis so – she is taken – I have beauties which my false glass at home did not discover.

FLORINDA. This woman watches me so, I shall get no opportunity to discover myself to him, and so miss the intent of my coming. (*Looking in* [BELVILE's] *hand*.) – But as I was saying, sir – by this line you should be a lover.

BELVILE. I thought how right you guessed, all men are in love, or pretend to be so. – Come, let me go; I'm weary of this fooling.

Walks away.

FLORINDA. I will not till you have confessed whether the passion that you have vowed Florinda be true or false.

She holds him; he strives to get from her.

BELVILE (*turns quick towards her*). Florinda!

FLORINDA. Softly.

BELVILE. Thou hast named one will fix me here for ever.

FLORINDA. She'll be disappointed then, who expects you this night at the garden gate, and if you fail not – as let me see the other hand – you will go near to do, she vows to die or make you happy.

Looks on CALLIS, *who observes 'em.*

BELVILE. What canst thou mean?

FLORINDA. That which I say. – Farewell.

Offers to go.

BELVILE. Oh charming sybil, stay, complete that joy, which, as it is, will turn into distraction! – Where must I be? At the garden gate? I know it – at night, you say – I'll sooner forfeit Heaven than disobey.

Enter DON PEDRO *and other maskers, and pass over the stage.*

CALLIS. Madam, your brother's here.

FLORINDA. Take this to instruct you farther.

Gives [BELVILE] *a letter, and goes off.*

FREDERICK. Have a care, sir, what you promise; this may be a trap laid by her brother to ruin you.

BELVILE. Do not disturb my happiness with doubts.

Opens the letter.

WILLMORE [*to* HELLENA]. My dear pretty creature, a thousand blessings on thee; still in this habit, you say, and after dinner at this place.

HELLENA. Yes, if you will swear to keep your heart, and not bestow it between this and that.

WILLMORE. By all the little gods of love I swear, I'll leave it with you; and if you run away with it, those deities of justice will revenge me.

Exeunt all the women [except LUCETTA].

FREDERICK. Do you know the hand?

BELVILE. 'Tis Florinda's. All blessings fall upon the virtuous maid.

FREDERICK. Nay, no idolatry, a sober sacrifice I'll allow you.

BELVILE. Oh friends, the welcom'st news, the softest letter! – Nay, you shall all see it; and could you now be serious, I might be made the happiest man the sun shines on!

WILLMORE. The reason of this mighty joy?

BELVILE. See how kindly she invites me to deliver her from the threatened violence of her brother – will you not assist me?

WILLMORE. I know not what thou mean'st, but I'll make one at any mischief where a woman's concerned. – But she'll be grateful to us for the favour, will she not?

BELVILE. How mean you?

WILLMORE. How should I mean? Thou know'st there's but one way for a woman to oblige me.

BELVILE. Do not profane – the maid is nicely virtuous.

WILLMORE. Who, pox, then she's fit for nothing but a husband. Let her e'en go, Colonel.

FREDERICK. Peace, she's the Colonel's mistress, sir.

WILLMORE. Let her be the devil; if she be thy mistress, I'll serve her – name the way.

BELVILE. Read here this postscript.

Gives him a letter.

WILLMORE (*reads*). 'At ten at night at the garden gate – of which, if I cannot get the key, I will contrive a way over the wall – come attended with a friend or two.' Kind heart, if we three cannot weave a string to let her down a garden wall, 'twere pity but the hangman wove one for us all.

FREDERICK. Let her alone for that; your woman's wit, your fair kind woman, will out-trick a broker or a Jew, and contrive like a Jesuit in chains. – But see, Ned Blunt is stol'n out after the lure of a damsel.

Exeunt BLUNT *and* LUCETTA.

BELVILE. So he'll scarce find his way home again unless we get him cried by the bellman in the market-place. And 'twould sound prettily – a lost English boy of thirty.

FREDERICK. I hope 'tis some common crafty sinner, one that will fit him. It may be she'll sell him for Peru, the rogue's sturdy and would work well in a mine. At least I hope she'll dress him for our mirth; cheat him of all, then have him well-favour'dly banged, and turned out naked at midnight.

WILLMORE. Prithee what humour is he of, that you wish him so well?

BELVILE. Why, of an English elder brother's humour, educated in a nursery, with a maid to tend him till fifteen, and lies with his grandmother till he's of age; one that knows no pleasure beyond riding to the next fair, or going up to London with his right worshipful father in parliament-time; wearing gay clothes, or making honourable love to his lady mother's laundry-maid; gets drunk at a hunting-match, and ten to one then gives some proofs of his prowess. – A pox upon him, he's our banker, and has all our cash about him; and if he fail, we are all broke.

FREDERICK. Oh let him alone for that matter, he's of a damned stingy quality, that will secure our stock. I know not in what danger it were indeed if the jilt should pretend she's in love with him, for 'tis a kind believing coxcomb; otherwise if he part with more than a piece of eight – geld him: for which offer he may chance to be beaten if she be a whore of the first rank.

BELVILE. Nay the rogue will not be easily beaten, he's stout enough. Perhaps if they talk beyond his capacity, he may chance to exercise his courage upon some of them; else I'm sure they'll find it as difficult to beat as to please him.

WILLMORE. 'Tis a lucky devil to light upon so kind a wench!

FREDERICK. Thou hadst a great deal of talk with thy little gipsy, couldst thou do no good upon her? For mine was hard-hearted.

WILLMORE. Hang her, she was some damned honest person of quality, I'm sure, she was so very free and witty. If her face be but answerable to her wit and humour, I would be bound to constancy this month to gain her. In the mean time, have you made no kind acquaintance since you came to town? – You do not use to be honest so long, gentlemen.

FREDERICK. Faith, love has kept us honest, we have been all fired with a beauty newly come to town, the famous Paduana Angellica Bianca.

WILLMORE. What, the mistress of the dead Spanish General?

BELVILE. Yes, she's now the only adored beauty of all the youth in Naples, who put on all their charms to appear lovely in her sight, their coaches, liveries, and themselves, all gay, as on a monarch's birthday, to attract the eyes of this fair charmer, while she has the pleasure to behold all languish for her that see her.

FREDERICK. 'Tis pretty to see with how much love the men regard her, and how much envy the women.

WILLMORE. What gallant has she?

BELVILE. None, she's exposed to sale, and four days in the week she's yours – for so much a month.

WILLMORE. The very thought of it quenches all manner of fire in me – yet prithee let's see her.

BELVILE. Let's first to dinner, and after that we'll pass the day as you please – but at night ye must all be at my devotion.

WILLMORE. I will not fail you.

[*Exeunt.*]

Act II, Scene i

The long street. Enter BELVILE *and* FREDERICK *in masking habits, and* WILLMORE *in his own clothes, with a vizard in his hand.*

WILLMORE. But why thus disguised and muzzled?

BELVILE. Because whatever extravagances we commit in these faces, our own may not be obliged to answer 'em.

WILLMORE. I should have changed my eternal buff too; but no matter, my little gipsy would not have found me out then: for if she should change hers, it is impossible I should know her, unless I should hear her prattle. A pox on't, I cannot get her out of my head. Pray Heaven, if ever I do see her again, she prove damnably ugly, that I may fortify myself against her tongue.

BELVILE. Have a care of love, for o' my conscience she was not of a quality to give thee any hopes.

WILLMORE. Pox on 'em, why do they draw a man in then? She has played with my heart so, that 'twill never lie still till I have met with some kind wench, that will play the game out with me. – Oh for my arms full of soft, white, kind – woman! Such as I fancy Angellica.

BELVILE. This is her house, if you were but in stock to get admittance; they have not dined yet; I perceive the picture is not out.

Enter BLUNT.

WILLMORE. I long to see the shadow of the fair substance, a man may gaze on that for nothing.

BLUNT. Colonel, thy hand – and thine, Fred. I have been an ass, a deluded fool, a very coxcomb from my birth till this hour, and heartily repent my little faith.

BELVILE. What the devil's the matter with thee, Ned?

[BLUNT]. Oh, such a mistress, Fred, such a girl!

WILLMORE. Ha! Where?

FREDERICK. Ay, where?

[BLUNT]. So fond, so amorous, so toying, and so fine! And all for sheer love, ye rogue! Oh, how she looked and kissed! And soothed my heart from my bosom! I cannot think I was awake, and yet methinks I see and feel her charms still. – Fred – try if she have not left the taste of her balmy kisses upon my lips –

Kisses him.

BELVILE. Ha! Ha! Ha!

WILLMORE. Death man, where is she?

[BLUNT]. What a dog was I to stay in dull England so long. – How have I laughed at the Colonel when he sighed for love! But now the little archer has revenged him, and by this one dart I can guess at all his joys, which then I took for fancies, mere dreams and fables. Well, I'm resolved to sell all in Essex, and plant here forever.

BELVILE. What a blessing 'tis, thou hast a mistress thou dar'st boast of; for I know thy humour is rather to have a proclaimed clap than a secret amour.

WILLMORE. Dost know her name?

BLUNT. Her name? No, 'sheartlikins: what care I for names? She's fair, young, brisk and kind, even to ravishment: and what a pox care I for knowing her by any other title?

WILLMORE. Didst give her anything?

BLUNT. Give her! – Ha, ha, ha! Why, she's a person of quality. – That's a good one, give her! 'Sheartlikins, dost think such creatures are to be bought? Or are we provided for such a purchase? Give her, quoth ye? Why, she presented me with this bracelet, for the toy of a diamond I used to wear. No, gentlemen, Ned Blunt is not every body. – She expects me again to-night.

WILLMORE. Egad, that's well; we'll all go.

BLUNT. Not a soul: no, gentlemen, you are wits; I am a dull country rogue, I.

FREDERICK. Well, sir, for all your person of quality, I shall be very glad to understand your purse be secure; 'tis our whole estate at present, which we are loath to hazard in one bottom: come sir, unlade.

BLUNT. Take the necessary trifle, useless now to me, that am beloved by such a gentlewoman. – 'Sheartlikins, money! Here, take mine too.

FREDERICK. No, keep that to be cozened, that we may laugh.

WILLMORE. Cozened! – Death! Would I could meet with one that would cozen me of all the love I could spare tonight.

FREDERICK. Pox 'tis some common whore upon my life.

BLUNT. A whore! Yes, with such clothes, such jewels, such a house, such furniture, and so attended! A whore!

BELVILE. Why yes, sir, they are whores, though they'll neither entertain you with drinking, swearing, or bawdry; are whores in all those gay clothes and right jewels; are whores with those great houses richly furnished with velvet beds, store of plate, handsome attendance, and fine coaches, are whores, and arrant ones.

WILLMORE. Pox on't, where do these fine whores live?

BELVILE. Where no rogues in office ycleped constables dare give 'em laws, nor the wine-inspired bullies of the town break their windows; yet they are whores, though this Essex calf believe 'em persons of quality.

BLUNT. 'Sheartlikins, y'are all fools, there are things about this Essex calf that shall take with the ladies, beyond all your wit and parts. – This shape and size, gentlemen, are not to be despised; my waist too, tolerably long, with other inviting signs, that shall be nameless.

WILLMORE. Egad I believe he may have met with some person of quality that may be kind to him.

BELVILE. Dost thou perceive any such tempting things about him that should make a fine woman, and of quality, pick him out from all mankind, to throw away her youth and beauty upon, nay, and her dear heart, too? – No, no, Angellica has raised the price too high.

WILLMORE. May she languish for mankind till she die, and be damned for that one sin alone.

Enter two BRAVOS *and hang up a great picture of Angellica's against the balcony, and two little ones at each side of the door.*

BELVILE. See there the fair sign to the inn, where a man may lodge that's fool enough to give her price.

WILLMORE *gazes on the picture.*

BLUNT. 'Sheartlikins, gentlemen, what's this?

BELVILE. A famous courtesan that's to be sold.

BLUNT. How! To be sold! Nay then I have nothing to say to her. – Sold! What impudence is practised in this country? – With what order and decency whoring's established here by virtue of the Inquisition. – Come, let's be gone, I'm sure we're no chapmen for this commodity.

FREDERICK. Thou art none, I'm sure, unless thou couldst have her in thy bed at a price of a coach in the street.

WILLMORE. How wondrous fair she is – a thousand crowns a month – by Heaven, as many kingdoms were too little. A plague of this poverty – of which I ne'er complain, but when it hinders my approach to beauty, which virtue ne'er could purchase.

Turns from the picture.

BLUNT. What's this? (*Reads.*) 'A thousand crowns a month!' – 'Sheartlikins, here's a sum! Sure 'tis a mistake. [*To a* BRAVO.] Hark you, friend, does she take or give so much by the month?

FREDERICK. A thousand crowns! Why, 'tis a portion for the Infanta.

BLUNT. Hark ye, friends, won't she trust?

BRAVO. This is a trade, sir, that cannot live by credit.

Enter DON PEDRO *in masquerade, followed by* STEPHANO.

BELVILE. See, here's more company; let's walk off a while.

Exeunt English. PEDRO *reads. Enter* ANGELLICA *and* MORETTA *in the balcony, and draw a silk curtain.*

PEDRO. Fetch me a thousand crowns, I never wished to buy this beauty at an easier rate.

Passes off.

ANGELLICA. Prithee what said those fellows to thee?

BRAVO. Madam, the first were admirers of beauty only, but no purchasers; they were merry with your price and picture, laughed at the sum, and so passed off.

ANGELLICA. No matter, I'm not displeased with their rallying; their wonder feeds my vanity, and he that wishes but to buy, gives me more pride than he that gives my price can make my pleasure.

BRAVO. Madam, the last I knew through all his disguises to be Don Pedro, nephew to the general, and who was with him in Pamplona.

ANGELLICA. Don Pedro! My old gallant's nephew! When his uncle died, he left him a vast sum of money; it is he who was so in love with me at Padua, and who used to make the general so jealous.

MORETTA. Is this he that used to prance before our window, and take such care to show himself an amorous ass? If I am not mistaken, he is the likeliest man to give your price.

ANGELLICA. The man is brave and generous, but of an humour so uneasy and inconstant that the victory over his heart is as soon lost as won; a slave that can add little to the triumph of the conqueror: but inconstancy's the sin of all mankind, therefore I'm resolved that nothing but gold shall charm my heart.

MORETTA. I'm glad on't; 'tis only interest that women of our profession ought to consider, though I wonder what has kept you from that general disease of our sex so long, I mean that of being in love.

ANGELLICA. A kind, but sullen star, under which I had the happiness to be born; yet I have had no time for love; the bravest and noblest of mankind have purchased my favours at so dear a rate, as if no coin but gold were current with our trade. – But here's Don Pedro again; fetch me my lute – for 'tis for him or Don Antonio the Viceroy's son, that I have spread my nets.

Enter at one door DON PEDRO [*and*] STEPHANO; DON ANTONIO *and* DIEGO *at the other door, with people following him in masquerade, antickly attired, some with music: they both go up to the picture.*

ANTONIO. A thousand crowns! Had not the painter flattered her, I should not think it dear.

PEDRO. Flattered her? By Heaven he cannot. I have seen the original, nor is there one charm here more than adorns her face and eyes; all this soft and sweet, with a certain languishing air, that no artist can represent.

ANTONIO. What I heard of her beauty before had fired my soul, but this confirmation of it has blown it to a flame.

PEDRO. Ha!

PAGE. Sir, I have known you throw away a thousand crowns on a worse face, and though y'are near your marriage, you may venture a little love here; Florinda will not miss it.

PEDRO (*aside*). Ha! Florinda! Sure 'tis Antonio.

ANTONIO. Florinda! Name not those distant joys, there's not one thought of her will check my passion here.

PEDRO (*aside*). Florinda scorned! And all my hopes defeated of the possession of Angellica!

A noise of a lute above. ANTONIO *gazes up.*

Her injuries, by Heaven, he shall not boast of!

Song to a lute above.

SONG.

[I]

When Damon first began to love,
He languished in a soft desire,
And knew not how the gods to move,
To lessen or increase his fire.
For Caelia in her charming eyes
Wore all love's sweets, and all his cruelties.

II

But as beneath a shade he lay,
Weaving of flowers for Caelia's hair,
She chanced to lead her flock that way,
And saw the am'rous shepherd there.
She gazed around upon the place,
And saw the grove (resembling night)
To all the joys of love invite,
Whilst guilty smiles and blushes dressed her face.
At this the bashful youth all transport grew,
And with kind force he taught the virgin how
To yield what all his sighs could never do.

ANTONIO. By Heaven, she's charming fair!

ANGELLICA *throws open the curtains and bows to* ANTONIO,
who pulls off his vizard, and bows and blows up kisses. PEDRO
unseen looks in his face.

PEDRO (*aside*). 'Tis he, the false Antonio!

ANTONIO (*to the* BRAVO). Friend, where must I pay my
off'ring of love? My thousand crowns I mean.

PEDRO. That off'ring I have designed to make,
And yours will come too late.

ANTONIO. Prithee be gone, I shall grow angry else,
And then thou art not safe.

PEDRO. My anger may be fatal, sir, as yours;
And he that enters here may prove this truth.

ANTONIO. I know not who thou art, but I am sure thou'rt
worth my killing, for aiming at Angellica.

They draw and fight. Enter WILLMORE *and* BLUNT, *who
draw and part 'em.*

BLUNT. 'Sheartlikins, here's fine doings.

WILLMORE. Tilting for the wench, I'm sure – nay, gad, if that
would win her I have as good a sword as the best of ye. –

Put up – put up, and take another time and place, for this is
designed for lovers only.

They all put up.

PEDRO. We are prevented; dare you meet me tomorrow on
the Molo?

For I've a title to a better quarrel,
That of Florinda, in whose credulous heart
Thou'st made an int'rest, and destroyed my hopes.

ANTONIO. Dare!
I'll meet thee there as early as the day.

PEDRO. We will come thus disguised, that whosoever chance to
get the better, he may escape unknown.

ANTONIO. It shall be so.

Exeunt PEDRO *and* STEPHANO.

Who should this rival be? Unless the English Colonel, of whom
I've often heard Don Pedro speak; it must be he, and time he
were removed. who lays a claim to all my happiness.

WILLMORE *having gazed all this while on the picture, pulls down a
little one.*

WILLMORE. This posture's loose and negligent,
The sight on't would beget a warm desire
In souls, whom impotence and age had chilled.
– This must along with me.

BRAVO. What means this rudeness, sir? – Restore the picture.

ANTONIO. Ha! Rudeness committed to the fair Angellica! –
Restore the picture, sir.

WILLMORE. Indeed I will not, sir.

ANTONIO. By Heaven but you shall.

WILLMORE. Nay, do not show your sword; if you do, by this
dear beauty – I will show mine too.

ANTONIO. What right can you pretend to't?

WILLMORE. That of possession which I will maintain – you perhaps have a thousand crowns to give for the original.

ANTONIO. No matter, sir, you shall restore the picture.

ANGELLICA and MORETTA *above.*

ANGELLICA. Oh, Moretta! What's the matter?

ANTONIO [*to* WILLMORE]. Or leave your life behind.

WILLMORE. Death! You lie – I will do neither.

They fight, the Spaniards join with ANTONIO, BLUNT *laying on like mad.*

ANGELLICA. Hold, I command you, if for me you fight.

They leave off and bow.

WILLMORE. How heavenly fair she is! – Ah plague of her price.

ANGELLICA. You sir in buff, you that appear a soldier, that first began this insolence –

WILLMORE. 'Tis true, I did so, if you call it insolence for a man to preserve himself; I saw your charming picture, and was wounded; quite through my soul each pointed beauty ran; and wanting a thousand crowns to procure my remedy, I laid this little picture to my bosom – which if you cannot allow me, I'll resign.

ANGELLICA. No, you may keep the trifle.

ANTONIO. You shall first ask me leave, and this.

[They] fight again as before. Enter BELVILE *and* FREDERICK *who join with the English.*

ANGELLICA. Hold! Will you ruin me! – Biskey, Sebastian, part 'em!

The SPANIARDS *are beaten off.*

MORETTA. Oh madam, we're undone, a pox upon that rude fellow, he's set on to ruin us: we shall never see good days till all these fighting poor rogues are sent to the galleys.

Enter BELVILE, BLUNT, FREDERICK *and* WILLMORE *with his shirt bloody.*

BLUNT. 'Sheartlikins, beat me at this sport, and I'll ne'er wear sword more.

BELVILE (*to* WILLMORE). The devil's in thee for a mad fellow, thou art always one at an unlucky adventure. – Come, let's be gone whilst we're safe, and remember these are Spaniards, a sort of people that know how to revenge an affront.

FREDERICK. You bleed; I hope you are not wounded.

WILLMORE. Not much. – A plague on your Dons, if they fight no better they'll ne'er recover Flanders. – What the devil was't to them that I took down the picture?

BLUNT. Took it! 'Sheartlikins, we'll have the great one too; 'tis ours by conquest. – Prithee help me up and I'll pull it down –

ANGELLICA. Stay, sir, and ere you affront me farther, let me know how you durst commit this outrage – to you I speak, sir, for you appear a gentleman.

WILLMORE. To me, madam? – Gentlemen, your servant.

BELVILE *stays him.*

BELVILE. Is the devil in thee? Dost know the danger of ent'ring the house of an incensed courtesan?

WILLMORE. I thank you for your care – but there are other matters in hand, there are, though we have no great temptation. – Death! Let me go.

FREDERICK. Yes, to your lodging, if you will, but not in here. – Damn these gay harlots. – By this hand I'll have as sound and handsome a whore for a patacoon. – Death, man, she'll murder thee.

WILLMORE. Oh, fear me not, shall I not venture where a beauty calls? A lovely charming beauty? For fear of danger! When by Heaven there's none so great as to long for her, whilst I want money to purchase her.

FREDERICK. Therefore 'tis loss of time, unless you had the thousand crowns to pay.

WILLMORE. It may be she may give a favour, at least I shall have the pleasure of saluting her when I enter, and when I depart.

BELVILE. Pox, she'll as soon lie with thee, as kiss thee, and sooner stab than do either – you shall not go.

ANGELLICA. Fear not, sir, all I have to wound with, is my eyes.

BLUNT. Let him go, 'sheartlikins, I believe the gentlewoman means well.

BELVILE. Well, take thy fortune, we'll expect you in the next street. – Farewell fool – farewell –

WILLMORE. B'ye, Colonel –

Goes in.

FREDERICK. The rogue's stark mad for a wench.

Exeunt.

Act II, Scene ii

A fine chamber.

Enter WILLMORE, ANGELLICA, *and* MORETTA.

ANGELLICA. Insolent sir, how durst you pull down my picture?

WILLMORE. Rather, how durst you set it up, to tempt poor
am'rous mortals with so much excellence? Which I find you
have but too well consulted by the unmerciful price you set
upon't. – Is all this heaven of beauty shown to move despair
in those that cannot buy? And can you think th'effects of
that despair should be less extravagant than I have shown?

ANGELLICA. I sent for you to ask my pardon, sir, not to
aggravate your crime. – I thought I should have seen you
at my feet imploring it.

WILLMORE. You are deceived. I came to rail at you, and rail
such truths, too, as shall let you see the vanity of that pride,
which taught you how to set such price on sin. For such it is,
whilst that which is love's due is meanly bartered for.

ANGELLICA. Ha, ha, ha, alas, good captain, what pity 'tis
your edifying doctrine will do no good upon me. – Moretta,
fetch the gentleman a glass, and let him survey himself, to
see what charms he has, (*Aside, in a soft tone.*) – and guess my
business.

MORETTA. He knows himself of old, I believe those breeches
and he have been acquainted ever since he was beaten at
Worcester.

ANGELLICA. Nay, do not abuse the poor creature –

MORETTA. Good weather-beaten Corporal, will you march off?
We have no need of your doctrine, though you have of our
charity; but at present we have no scraps; we can afford no
kindness for God's sake; in fine, sirrah, the price is too high
i'th' mouth for you, therefore troop, I say.

WILLMORE [*giving money to* MORETTA]. Here, good fore-
woman of the shop, serve me, and I'll be gone.

MORETTA. Keep it to pay your laundress, your linen stinks of
the gun-room; for here's no selling by retail.

WILLMORE. Thou hast sold plenty of thy stale ware at a
cheap rate.

MORETTA. Ay, the more silly kind heart I, but this is an age
wherein beauty is at higher rates. In fine, you know the
price of this.

WILLMORE. I grant you 'tis here set down a thousand crowns
a month. − Pray, how much may come to my share for
a pistole? Bawd, take your black-lead and sum it up, that
I may have a pistole's worth of this vain gay thing, and
I'll trouble you no more.

MORETTA. Pox on him, he'll fret me to death. Abominable
fellow, I tell thee, we only sell by the whole piece.

WILLMORE. 'Tis very hard, the whole cargo or nothing. −
Faith, madam, my stock will not reach it, I cannot be your
chapman. −Yet I have countrymen in town, merchants of
love, like me; I'll see if they'll put in for a share, we cannot
lose much by it, and what we have no use for, we'll sell upon
the Friday's mart, at 'Who gives more?' I am studying,
madam, how to purchase you, though at present I am
unprovided of money.

ANGELLICA. Sure, this from any other man would anger me −
nor shall he know the conquest he has made. [*To*
WILLMORE.] − Poor angry man, how I despise this railing.

WILLMORE. Yes, I am poor − but I'm a gentleman,
And one that scorns this baseness which you practise.
Poor as I am, I would not sell my self.
No, not to gain your charming high-prized person.
Though I admire you strangely for your beauty,

Yet I condemn your mind.
- And yet I would at any rate enjoy you;
At your own rate - but cannot. - See here
The only sum I can command on earth;
I know not where to eat when this is gone:
Yet such a slave I am to love and beauty,
This last reserve I'll sacrifice to enjoy you.
- Nay, do not frown; I know you're to be bought,
And would be bought by me, by me,
For a mean trifling sum, if I could pay it down.
Which happy knowledge I will still repeat,
And lay it to my heart: it has a virtue in't,
And soon will cure those wounds your eyes have made.
- And yet - there's something so divinely powerful there -
Nay, I will gaze - to let you see my strength.

Holds her, looks on her, and pauses and sighs.

By Heaven, bright creature, I would not for the world
Thy fame were half so fair as is thy face.

Turns her away from him.

ANGELLICA (*aside*). His words go through me to the very soul.
[*To him.*] - If you have nothing else to say to me.

WILLMORE. Yes, you shall hear how infamous you are -
For which I do not hate thee:
But that secures my heart, and all the flames it feels
Are but so many lusts,
I know it by their sudden bold intrusion.
The fire's impatient and betrays, 'tis false -
For had it been the purer flame of love,
I should have pined and languished at your feet,
Ere found the impudence to have discovered it.
I now dare stand your scorn, and your denial.

MORETTA. Sure she's bewitched, that she can stand thus
tamely, and hear his saucy railing. Sirrah, will you be gone?

ANGELLICA (*to* MORETTA). How dare you take this liberty!
Withdraw. – Pray tell me, sir, are not you guilty of the same
mercenary crime? When a lady is proposed to you for a wife,
you never ask how fair, discreet, or virtuous she is; but what's
her fortune – which, if but small, you cry, 'She will not do my
business' – and basely leave her, though she languish for you. –
Say, is not this as poor?

WILLMORE. It is a barbarous custom, which I will scorn to
defend in our sex, and do despise in yours.

ANGELLICA. Thou'rt a brave fellow! Put up thy gold,
and know,
That were thy fortune large, as is thy soul,
Thou shouldst not buy my love,
Couldst thou forget those mean effects of vanity
Which set me out to sale; and, as a lover,
Prize my yielding joys.
Canst thou believe they'll be entirely thine,
Without considering they were mercenary?

WILLMORE (*aside*). I cannot tell; I must bethink me first – ha,
death, I'm going to believe her.

ANGELLICA. Prithee, confirm that faith – or if thou canst not –
flatter me a little, 'twill please me from thy mouth.

WILLMORE (*aside*). Curse on thy charming tongue! Dost
thou return
My feigned contempt with so much subtlety?
[*To her.*] Thou'st found the easiest way into my heart, Though I
yet know that all thou say'st is false.

Turns from her in rage.

ANGELLICA. By all that's good 'tis real,
I never loved before, though oft a mistress.
– Shall my first vows be slighted?

WILLMORE (*aside*). What can she mean?

ANGELLICA (*in an angry tone*). I find you cannot credit me.

WILLMORE. I know you take me for an arrant ass,
An ass that may be soothed into belief,
And then be used at pleasure.
– But, madam I have been so often cheated
By perjured, soft, deluding hypocrites,
That I've no faith left for the cozening sex,
Especially for women of your trade.

ANGELLICA. The low esteem you have of me, perhaps
May bring my heart again:
For I have pride that yet surmounts my love.

She turns with pride, he holds her.

WILLMORE. Throw off this pride, this enemy to bliss,
And show the power of love: 'tis with those arms
I can be only vanquished, made a slave.

ANGELLICA. Is all my mighty expectation vanished?
– No, I will not hear thee talk – thou hast a charm
In every word, that draws my heart away.
And all the thousand trophies I designed
Thou hast undone. – Why art thou soft?
Thy looks are bravely rough, and meant for war.
Could'st thou not storm on still?
I then, perhaps, had been as free as thou.

WILLMORE (*aside*). Death! How she throws her fire about
my soul!
[*To her.*] Take heed, fair creature, how you raise my hopes,
Which once assumed pretend to all dominion.
There's not a joy thou hast in store
I shall not then command:
For which I'll pay thee back my soul, my life,
Come, let's begin th'account this happy minute.

ANGELLICA. And will you pay me then the price I ask?

WILLMORE. Oh, why dost thou draw me from an awful
    worship,
    By showing thou art no divinity?
    Conceal the fiend, and show me all the angel;
    Keep me but ignorant, and I'll be devout,
    And pay my vows forever at this shrine.

Kneels and kisses her hand.

ANGELLICA. The pay I mean is but thy love for mine.
    – Can you give that?

WILLMORE. Entirely – come, let's withdraw: where I'll renew
    my vows – and breathe 'em with such ardour, thou shalt not
    doubt my zeal.

ANGELLICA. Thou hast a power too strong to be resisted.

Exeunt WILLMORE *and* ANGELLICA.

MORETTA. Now my curse go with you. – Is all our project
    fallen to this? To love the only enemy to our trade? Nay, to
    love such a shameroon, a very beggar; nay, a pirate-beggar,
    whose business is to rifle and be gone, a no-purchase, no-pay
    tatterdemalion, and English picaroon; a rogue that fights for
    daily drink, and takes a pride in being loyally lousy. – Oh, I
    could curse now, if I durst. – This is the fate of most whores.

    Trophies, which from believing fops we win,
    Are spoils to those who cozen us again.

    [*Exit.*]

Act III, Scene i

A street. Enter FLORINDA, VALERIA, HELLENA, *in antic different dresses from what they were in before,* CALLIS *attending.*

FLORINDA. I wonder what should make my brother in so ill a humour: I hope he has not found out our ramble this morning.

HELLENA. No, if he had, we should have heard on't at both ears, and have been mewed up this afternoon; which I would not for the world should have happened. – Hey ho! I'm as sad as a lover's lute.

VALERIA. Well, methinks we have learnt this trade of gipsies as readily as if we had been bred upon the road to Loretto: and yet I did so fumble, when I told the stranger his fortune, that I was afraid I should have told my own and yours by mistake. – But, methinks Hellena has been very serious ever since.

FLORINDA. I would give my garters she were in love, to be revenged upon her for abusing me. – How is't, Hellena?

HELLENA. Ah! – Would I had never seen my mad monsieur – and yet for all your laughing, I am not in love – and yet this small acquaintance, o' my conscience, will never out of my head.

VALERIA. Ha, ha, ha – I laugh to think how thou art fitted with a lover, a fellow that, I warrant, loves every new face he sees.

HELLENA. Hum – he has not kept his word with me here – and may be taken up – that thought is not very pleasant to me. – What the deuce should this be now that I feel?

VALERIA. What is't like?

HELLENA. Nay, the Lord knows – but if I should be hanged I cannot choose but be angry and afraid, when I think that mad fellow should be in love with anybody but me. – What to think of myself, I know not. – Would I could meet with some true damned gipsy that I might know my fortune.

VALERIA. Know it! Why there's nothing so easy. Thou wilt love this wandering inconstant till thou find'st thy self hanged about his neck, and then be as mad to get free again.

FLORINDA. Yes, Valeria; we shall see her bestride his baggage-horse and follow him to the campaign.

HELLENA. So, so; now you are provided for, there's no care taken of poor me. – But since you have set my heart awishing, I am resolved to know for what. I will not die of the pip, so I will not.

FLORINDA. Art thou mad to talk so? Who will like thee well enough to have thee, that hears what a mad wench thou art?

HELLENA. Like me! I don't intend every he that likes me shall have me, but he that I like: I should have stayed in the nunnery still, if I had liked my Lady Abbess as well as she liked me. No, I came thence, not (as my wise brother imagines) to take an eternal farewell of the world, but to love and to be beloved; and I will be beloved, or I'll get one of your men, so I will.

VALERIA. Am I put into the number of lovers?

HELLENA. You? Why coz, I know thou'rt too good natured to leave us in any design: thou wouldst venture a cast, though thou camest off a loser, especially with such a gamester. – I observe your man, and your willing ear incline that way; and if you are not a lover, 'tis an art soon learnt – that I find. (*Sighs.*)

FLORINDA. I wonder how you learnt to love so easily. I had a thousand charms to meet my eyes and ears, e'er I could yield, and 'twas the knowledge of Belvile's merit, not the surprising person, took my soul. – Thou art too rash, to give a heart at first sight.

HELLENA. Hang your considering lover; I never thought beyond the fancy that 'twas a very pretty, idle, silly kind of pleasure to pass one's time with: to write little, soft, nonsensical billets, and with great difficulty and danger receive answers, in which I shall have my beauty praised, my wit admired (though little or none) and have the vanity and power to know I am desirable; then I have the more inclination that way, because I am to be a nun, and so shall not be suspected to have any such earthly thoughts about me. – But when I walk thus – and sigh thus – they'll think my mind's upon my monastery, and cry, 'How happy 'tis she's so resolved!' – But not a word of man.

FLORINDA. What a mad creature's this?

HELLENA. I'll warrant, if my brother hears either of you sigh, he cries (gravely) 'I fear you have the indiscretion to be in love, but take heed of the honour of our house and your own unspotted fame'; and so he conjures on till he has laid the soft-winged god in your hearts, or broke the bird's nest. – But see here comes your lover: but where's my inconstant? Let's step aside, and we may learn something.

[*They*] *go aside. Enter* BELVILE, FREDERICK *and* BLUNT.

BELVILE. What means this? The picture's taken in.

BLUNT. It may be the wench is good-natured and will be kind gratis. Your friend's a proper handsome fellow.

BELVILE. I rather think she has cut his throat and is fled: I am mad he should throw himself into dangers. – Pox on't, I shall want him, too, at night. Let's knock and ask for him.

HELLENA. My heart goes a-pit a-pat, for fear 'tis my man they talk of.

[BELVILE and BLUNT] *knock;* MORETTA *above.*

MORETTA. What would you have?

BELVILE. Tell the stranger that entered here about two hours ago, that his friends stay here for him.

MORETTA. A curse upon him for Moretta, would he were at the devil – but he's coming to you.

[*Enter* WILLMORE.]

HELLENA. Aye, aye, 'tis he. Oh, how this vexes me.

BELVILE. And how, and how, dear lad, has fortune smiled? Are we to break her windows, or raise up altars to her, ha?

WILLMORE. Does not my fortune sit triumphant on my brow? Dost not see the little wanton god there, all gay and smiling? Have I not an air about my face and eyes that distinguish me from the crowd of common lovers? By Heaven, Cupid's quiver has not half so many darts as her eyes. – Oh, such a *bona roba*, to sleep in her arms is lying in fresco, all perfumed air about me.

HELLENA (*aside*). Here's fine encouragement for me to fool on.

WILLMORE. Hark'ee, where didst thou purchase that rich Canary we drank to-day? Tell me, that I may adore the spigot, and sacrifice to the butt: the juice was divine into which I must dip my rosary, and then bless all things that I would have bold or fortunate!

BELVILE. Well, sir, let's go take a bottle and hear the story of your success.

FREDERICK. Would not French wine do better?

WILLMORE. Damn the hungry balderdash; cheerful sack has a generous virtue in't, inspiring a successful confidence, gives eloquence to the tongue, and vigour to the soul, and has in a few hours completed all my hopes and wishes. There's nothing left to raise a new desire in me. – Come, let's be gay and wanton – and gentlemen, study, study what you want, for here are friends – that will supply, gentlemen [*He shows coins.*] Hark! What a charming sound they make! – 'Tis he and she gold whilst here, and shall beget new pleasures every moment.

BLUNT. But hark'ee, sir, you are not married, are you?

WILLMORE. All the honey of matrimony, but none of the sting, friend.

BLUNT. 'Sheartlikins, thou'rt a fortunate rogue.

WILLMORE. I am so, sir, let these inform you. – Ha, how sweetly they chime! Pox of poverty, it makes a man a slave, makes wit and honour sneak, my soul grew lean and rusty for want of credit.

BLUNT. 'Sheartlikins, this I like well; it looks like my lucky bargain! Oh, how I long for the approach of my squire, that is to conduct me to her house again. Why! Here's two provided for.

FREDERICK. By this light, y'are happy men.

BLUNT. Fortune is pleased to smile on us, gentlemen – to smile on us.

Enter SANCHO *and pulls down* BLUNT *by the sleeve.
They go aside.*

SANCHO. Sir, my lady expects you – she has removed all that might oppose your will and pleasure – and is impatient till you come.

BLUNT. Sir, I'll attend you. – Oh, the happiest rogue! I'll take no leave, lest they either dog me, or stay me.

Exit with SANCHO.

BELVILE. But then the little gipsy is forgot?

WILLMORE. A mischief on thee for putting her into my thoughts; I had quite forgot her else, and this night's debauch had drunk her quite down.

HELLENA. Had it so, good Captain?

Claps him on the back.

WILLMORE (*aside*). Ha! I hope she did not hear me.

HELLENA. What, afraid of such a champion?

WILLMORE. Oh! You're a fine lady of your word, are you not? To make a man languish a whole day –

HELLENA. In tedious search of me.

WILLMORE. Egad, child, thou'rt in the right, hadst thou seen what a melancholy dog I have been ever since I was a lover, how I have walked the streets like a Capuchin, with my hands in my sleeves – faith, sweetheart, thou wouldst pity me.

HELLENA [*aside*]. Now, if I should be hanged I can't be angry with him, he dissembles so heartily. – Alas, good Captain, what pains you have taken. – Now were I ungrateful not to reward so true a servant.

WILLMORE. Poor soul! That's kindly said, I see thou bearest a conscience – come then for a beginning, show me thy dear face.

HELLENA. I'm afraid, my small acquaintance, you have been staying that swinging stomach you boasted of this morning; I then remember my little collation would have gone down with you, without the sauce of a handsome face – is your stomach so queasy now?

WILLMORE. Faith, long fasting, child, spoils a man's appetite –
yet, if you durst treat, I could so lay about me still.

HELLENA. And would you fall to, before a priest says grace?

WILLMORE. Oh, fie, fie, what an old, out-of-fashioned thing
hast thou named? Thou couldst not dash me more out of
countenance, shouldst thou show me an ugly face.

Whilst he is seemingly courting HELLENA, *enter* ANGELLICA,
MORETTA, BISKEY, *and* SEBASTIAN, *all in masquerade:*
ANGELLICA *sees* WILLMORE *and stares.*

ANGELLICA. Heavens, 'tis he! And passionately fond to see
another woman!

MORETTA. What could you less expect from such a
swaggerer?

ANGELLICA. Expect? As much as I paid him – a heart entire
Which I had pride enough to think, when'er I gave,
It would have raised the man above the vulgar,
Made him all soul, and that all soft and constant.

HELLENA. You see, Captain, how willing I am to be friends
with you, till time and ill luck make us lovers; and ask you
the question first, rather than put your modesty to the blush,
by asking me: for alas, I know you captains are such strict
men, and such severe observers of your vows to chastity, that
'twill be hard to prevail with your tender conscience to
marry a young willing maid.

WILLMORE. Do not abuse me, for fear I should take thee at
thy word, and marry thee indeed, which I'm sure will be
revenge sufficient.

HELLENA. O' my conscience, that will be our destiny, because
we are both of one humour; I am as inconstant as you, for
I have considered, captain, that a handsome woman has
a great deal to do whilst her face is good, for then is our

harvest-time to gather friends; and should I in these days of
my youth, catch a fit of foolish constancy, I were undone; 'tis
loitering by day-light in our great journey. Therefore
I declare, I'll allow but one year for love, one year for
indifference, and one year for hate – and then – go hang
yourself – for I protest myself the gay, the kind, and the
inconstant – the devil's in't if this won't please you.

WILLMORE. Oh, most damnably! – I have a heart with a hole
quite through it too, no prison, mine, to keep a mistress in.

ANGELLICA (aside). Perjured man! How I believe thee now.

HELLENA. Well, I see our business as well as humours are
alike, yours to cozen as many maids as will trust you, and
I as many men as have faith. – See if I have not as desperate
a lying look, as you can have for the heart of you.

Pulls off her vizard; he starts.

– How do you like it, captain?

WILLMORE. Like it! By Heaven, I never saw so much beauty!
Oh the charms of those sprightly black eyes, that strangely
fair face, full of smiles and dimples! Those soft, round,
melting cherry lips and small even white teeth! – Not to be
expressed, but silently adored! – Oh, one look more, and
strike me dumb, or I shall repeat nothing else till I'm mad.

He seems to court her to pull off her vizard: she refuses.

ANGELLICA. I can endure no more – nor is it fit to interrupt
him; for if I do, my jealousy has so destroyed my reason,
I shall undo him – therefore I'll retire. And you Sebastian (*To
one of her* BRAVOS.) follow that woman, and learn who 'tis;
while you (*To the other* BRAVO.) tell the fugitive, I would
speak to him instantly.

Exit. This while FLORINDA [*vizarded*] *is talking to* BELVILE,
who stands sullenly. FREDERICK *courting* VALERIA.

VALERIA. Prithee, dear stranger, be not so sullen, for though you have lost your love, you see my friend frankly offers you hers, to play with in the mean time.

BELVILE. Faith, madam, I am sorry I can't play at her game.

FREDERICK. Pray leave your intercession and mind your own affair, they'll better agree apart; he's a modest sigher in company, but alone no woman 'scapes him.

FLORINDA. Sure, he does but rally – yet if it should be true – I'll tempt him farther. [*To* BELVILE.] Believe me, noble stranger, I'm no common mistress. And for a little proof on't – wear this jewel – nay, take it, sir, 'tis right, and bills of exchange may sometimes miscarry.

BELVILE. Madam, why am I chose out of all mankind to be the object of your bounty?

VALERIA. There's another civil question asked.

FREDERICK. Pox of's modesty, it spoils his own markets, and hinders mine.

FLORINDA. Sir, from my window I have often seen you; and women of my quality have so few opportunities for love, that we ought to lose none.

FREDERICK. Ay, this is something! Here's a woman! – When shall I be blessed with so much kindness from your fair mouth? (*Aside to* BELVILE.) – Take the jewel, fool.

BELVILE. You tempt me strangely, madam, every way.

FLORINDA (*aside*). So, if I find him false, my whole repose is gone.

BELVILE. And but for a vow I've made to a very fair lady, this goodness had subdued me.

FREDERICK [*to* BELVILE]. Pox on't be kind, in pity to me be kind, for I am to thrive here but as you treat her friend.

HELLENA [*to* WILLMORE]. Tell me what you did in yonder house, and I'll unmask.

WILLMORE. Yonder house – oh – I went to – a – to – why, there's a friend of mine lives there.

HELLENA. What a she, or a he friend?

WILLMORE. A man upon honour! A man. – A she friend! No, no, madam, you have done my business, I thank you.

HELLENA. And was't your man friend that had more darts in's eyes than Cupid carries in's whole budget of arrows?

WILLMORE. So –

HELLENA. 'Ah such a *bona roba:* to be in her arms is lying in fresco, all perfumed air about me.' – Was this your man friend too?

WILLMORE. So –

HELLENA. That gave you the he, and the she-gold, that begets young pleasures?

WILLMORE. Well, well, madam, then you see there are ladies in the world, that will not be cruel – there are, madam, there are –

HELLENA. And there be men too as fine, wild, inconstant fellows as yourself, there be, Captain, there be, if you go to that now – therefore I'm resolved –

WILLMORE. Oh!

HELLENA. To see your face no more –

WILLMORE. Oh!

HELLENA. Till tomorrow.

WILLMORE. Egad you frighted me.

HELLENA. Nor then neither, unless you'll swear never to see that lady more.

WILLMORE. See her! – Why! Never to think of womankind again?

HELLENA. Kneel, and swear.

[WILLMORE] *kneels; she gives him her hand.*

WILLMORE. I do, never to think – to see – to love – nor lie with any but thy self.

HELLENA. Kiss the book.

WILLMORE Oh, most religiously.

Kisses her hand.

HELLENA. Now, what a wicked creature am I, to damn a proper fellow.

CALLIS (*to* FLORINDA). Madam, I'll stay no longer; 'tis e'en dark.

FLORINDA [*to* BELVILE]. However, sir, I'll leave this with you – that when I'm gone, you may repent the opportunity you have lost by your modesty.

Gives him the jewel, which is her picture, and exits. He gazes after her.

WILLMORE [*to* HELLENA]. 'Twill be an age till tomorrow – and till then I will most impatiently expect you. Adieu, my dear, pretty angel.

Exeunt all the women.

BELVILE. Ha! Florinda's picture! 'Twas she herself – what a dull dog was I? I would have given the world for one minute's discourse with her –

FREDERICK. This comes of your modesty. – Ah pox o' your vow, 'twas ten to one but we had lost the jewel by't.

BELVILE. Willmore! The blessed'st opportunity lost! – Florinda, friends, Florinda!

WILLMORE. Ah rogue! Such black eyes, such a face, such a mouth, such teeth – and so much wit!

BELVILE. All, all, and a thousand charms besides.

WILLMORE. Why, dost thou know her?

BELVILE. Know her! Ay, ay, and a pox take me with all my heart for being modest.

WILLMORE. But hark ye, friend of mine, are you my rival? And have I been only beating the bush all this while?

BELVILE. I understand thee not – I'm mad – see here –

Shows the picture [of FLORINDA].

WILLMORE. Ha! Whose picture's this? – 'Tis a fine wench!

FREDERICK. The Colonel's mistress, sir.

WILLMORE. Oh, oh, here – I thought it had been another prize – come, come, a bottle will set thee right again.

Gives the picture back.

BELVILE. I am content to try, and by that time 'twill be late enough for our design.

WILLMORE. Agreed.

Love does all day the soul's great empire keep,
But wine at night lulls the soft god asleep.

Exeunt.

Act III, Scene ii

Lucetta's house. Enter BLUNT *and* LUCETTA *with a light.*

LUCETTA. Now we are safe and free, no fears of the coming home of my old jealous husband, which made me a little thoughtful when you came in first – but now love is all the business of my soul.

BLUNT (*aside*). I am transported. – Pox on't, that I had but some fine things to say to her, such as lovers use – I was a fool not to learn of Fred a little by heart before I came. – Something I must say. [*To her.*] 'Sheartlikins, sweet soul! I am not used to compliment, but I'm an honest gentleman, and thy humble servant.

LUCETTA. I have nothing to pay for so great a favour, but such a love as cannot but be great, since at first sight of that sweet face and shape it made me your absolute captive.

BLUNT (*aside*). Kind heart, how prettily she talks! Egad I'll show her husband a Spanish trick; send him out of the world, and marry her: she's damnably in love with me, and will ne'er mind settlements, and so there's that saved.

LUCETTA. Well, sir, I'll go and undress me, and be with you instantly.

BLUNT. Make haste then, for 'dsheartlikins, dear soul, thou canst not guess at the pain of a longing lover when his joys are drawn within the compass of a few minutes.

LUCETTA. You speak my sense, and I'll make haste to prove it.

Exit.

BLUNT. 'Tis a rare girl, and this one night's enjoyment with her will be worth all the days I ever passed in Essex. – Would she would go with me into England, though to say truth, there's plenty of whores already. – But a pox on 'em they are such mercenary prodigal whores, that they want such a one as this, that's free and generous, to give 'em good examples. – Why, what a house she has! How rich and fine!

Enter SANCHO.

SANCHO. Sir, my lady has sent me to conduct you to her chamber.

BLUNT. Sir, I shall be proud to follow. – Here's one of her
    servants too: 'sheartlikins, by this garb and gravity he might be
    a Justice of Peace in Essex, and is but a pimp here.

Exeunt.

Act III, Scene iii

The scene changes to a chamber with an alcove bed in it, a table, etc.,
LUCETTA in bed. Enter SANCHO and BLUNT, who takes the candle
of SANCHO at the door.

SANCHO. Sir, my commission reaches no farther.

BLUNT. Sir, I'll excuse your compliment. –

    [*Exit* SANCHO.]

    What, in bed, my sweet mistress?

LUCETTA. You see, I still out-do you in kindness.

BLUNT. And thou shalt see what haste I'll make to quit scores –
    oh, the luckiest rogue!

Undresses himself.

LUCETTA Should you be false or cruel now!

BLUNT. False, 'sheartlikins, what dost thou take me for a Jew?
    An insensible heathen. – A pox of thy old jealous husband:
    an' he were dead – egad, sweet soul, it should be none of
    my fault if I did not marry thee.

LUCETTA. It never should be mine.

BLUNT. Good soul, I'm the fortunatest dog!

LUCETTA. Are you not undressed yet?

BLUNT. As much as my impatience will permit.

Goes towards the bed in his shirt, drawers.

LUCETTA. Hold, sir, put out the light, it may betray us else.

BLUNT. Any thing, I need no other light but that of thine eyes! – (*Aside.*) 'Sheartlikins, there I think I had it.

Puts out the candle; the bed descends; he gropes about to find it.

Why – why – where am I got? What, not yet? – Where are you, sweetest? – Ah, the rogue's silent now – a pretty love-trick, this – how she'll laugh at me anon! – You need not, my dear rogue! You need not! I'm all on fire already – come, come, now call me in pity. – Sure, I'm enchanted! I have been round the chamber, and can find neither woman, nor bed. – I locked the door, I'm sure she cannot go that way; or if she could, the bed could not. – Enough, enough, my pretty wanton, do not carry the jest too far.

Lights on a trap, and is let down.

Ha, betrayed! Dogs! Rogues! Pimps! Help! Help!

Enter LUCETTA, PHILIPPO, *and* SANCHO *with a light.*

PHILIPPO Ha, ha, ha! He's dispatched finely.

LUCETTA. Now, sir, had I been coy, we had missed of this booty.

PHILIPPO. Nay when I saw 'twas a substantial fool, I was mollified; but when you dote upon a serenading coxcomb, upon a face, fine clothes, and a lute, it makes me rage.

LUCETTA. You know I was never guilty of that folly, my dear Philippo, but with your self – but come, let's see what we have got by this.

PHILIPPO. A rich coat! – Sword and hat! – These breeches too – are well-lined! – See here a gold watch! – A purse – Ha! Gold! – At least two hundred pistoles! A bunch of diamond rings; and one with the family arms! – A gold box, with a medal of his king! And his lady mother's picture! – These were sacred relics, believe me! – See, the waistband of his breeches have a mine of gold! – Old Queen Bess's! We have a quarrel to her ever since eighty-eight, and may therefore justify the theft, the Inquisition might have committed it.

LUCETTA. See, a bracelet of bowed gold, these, his sisters tied about his arm at parting – but well – for all this, I fear his being a stranger may make a noise, and hinder our trade with them hereafter.

PHILIPPO. That's our security; he is not only a stranger to us, but to the country, too – the common shore into which he is descended, thou know'st, conducts him into another street, which this light will hinder him from ever finding again – he knows neither your name, nor that of the street where your house is, nay, nor the way to his own lodgings.

LUCETTA. And art not thou an unmerciful rogue, not to afford him one night for all this? – I should not have been such a Jew.

PHILIPPO. Blame me not, Lucetta, to keep as much of thee as I can to my self – come, that thought makes me wanton – let's to bed – Sancho, lock up these.

This is the fleece which fools do bear,
Designed for witty men to shear.

Exeunt.

Act III, Scene iv

The scene changes, and discovers BLUNT *creeping out of a common shore, his face, etc., all dirty.*

BLUNT (*climbing up*). Oh Lord! I am got out at last and (which is a miracle) without a clue – and now to damning and cursing – but if that would ease me, where shall I begin? With my fortune, my self, or the quean that cozened me? – What a dog was I to believe in woman! Oh coxcomb – ignorant conceited coxcomb! To fancy she could be enamoured with my person, at first sight enamoured. – Oh, I'm a cursed puppy, 'tis plain, 'fool' was writ upon my forehead, she perceived it – saw the Essex calf there – for what allurements could there be in this countenance, which I can endure because I'm acquainted with it. – Oh, dull silly dog! To be thus soothed into a cozening! Had I been drunk, I might fondly have credited the young quean! But as I was in my right wits, to be thus cheated, confirms it: I am a dull believing English country fop. – But my comrades! Death and the devil, there's the worst of all– then a ballad will be sung to-morrow on the Prado, to a lousy tune of the Enchanted Squire and the Annihilated Damsel. – But Fred, that rogue, and the Colonel, will abuse me beyond all Christian patience. – Had she left me my clothes, I have a bill of exchange at home would have saved my credit – but now all hope is taken from me. – Well, I'll home (if I can find the way) with this consolation, that I am not the first kind believing coxcomb; but there are, gallants, many such good natures amongst ye.

And though you've better arts to hide your follies, Adsheartlikins, y'are all as arrant cullies.

[*Exit.*]

Act III, Scene v

The garden, in the night. Enter FLORINDA *in an undress, with a key and a little box.*

FLORINDA. Well, thus far I'm in my way to happiness; I have got my self free from Callis; my brother too, I find by yonder light, is got into his cabinet, and thinks not of me. I have by good fortune got the key of the garden back-door. – I'll open it, to prevent Belvile's knocking – a little noise will now alarm my brother. Now am I as fearful as a young thief. (*Unlocks the door.*) – Hark – what noise is that? Oh, 'twas the wind that played amongst the boughs. – Belvile stays long, methinks – it's time – stay – for fear of a surprise, I'll hide these jewels in yonder jessamin.

She goes to lay down the box. Enter WILLMORE *drunk.*

WILLMORE. What the devil is become of these fellows, Belvile and Frederick? They promised to stay at the next corner for me, but who the devil knows the corner of a full moon? – Now – whereabouts am I? – hah – what have we here? A garden! – A very convenient place to sleep in – hah – what has God sent us here? A female – by this light, a woman; I'm a dog if it be not a very wench. –

FLORINDA. He's come! – Hah – who's there?

WILLMORE. Sweet soul, let me salute thy shoe-string!

FLORINDA. 'Tis not my Belvile. – Good Heavens, I know him not. – Who are you, and from whence come you?

WILLMORE. Prithee – prithee, child – not so many hard questions – let it suffice I am here, child. – Come, come kiss me.

FLORINDA. Good gods! What luck is mine?

WILLMORE. Only good luck, child, parlous good luck. – Come hither – 'tis a delicate, shining wench – by this hand, she's perfumed, and smells like any nosegay. – Prithee, dear soul, let's not play the fool and lose time – precious time – for as Gad shall save me, I'm as honest a fellow as breathes, though I'm a little disguised at present. – Come, I say – why, thou may'st be free with me, I'll be very secret. I'll not boast who 'twas obliged me, not I – for hang me if I know thy name.

FLORINDA. Heavens! What a filthy beast is this?

WILLMORE. I am so, and thou ought'st the sooner to lie with me for that reason. – For look you, child, there will be no sin in't, because 'twas neither designed nor premeditated; 'tis pure accident on both sides – that's a certain thing now. – Indeed, should I make love to you, and you vow fidelity – and swear and lie till you believed and yielded – that were to make it wilful fornication, the crying sin of the nation. – Thou art, therefore (as thou art a good Christian) obliged in conscience to deny me nothing. Now – come, be kind without any more idle prating.

FLORINDA. Oh, I am ruined – wicked man, unhand me.

WILLMORE. Wicked! Egad, child, a judge, were he young and vigorous, and saw those eyes of thine, would know 'twas they gave the first blow – the first provocation. – Come, prithee let's lose no time, I say – this is a fine, convenient place.

FLORINDA. Sir, let me go, I conjure you, or I'll call out.

WILLMORE. Ay, ay, you were best to call witness to see how finely you treat me – do –

FLORINDA. I'll cry murder, rape, or any thing if you do not instantly let me go!

WILLMORE. A rape! Come, come, you lie, you baggage, you lie. What, I'll warrant you would fain have the world believe now that you are not so forward as I. No, not you – why at this time of night was your cobweb-door set open, dear spider – but to catch flies? – Ha, come – or I shall be damnably angry. – Why, what a coil is here –

FLORINDA. Sir, can you think –

WILLMORE. That you would do't for nothing? Oh, oh, I find what you would be at – look here, here's a pistole for you – here's a work indeed – here – take it, I say –

FLORINDA. For Heaven's sake, sir, as you're a gentleman –

WILLMORE. So – now, now– she would be wheedling me for more – what, you will not take it then – you are resolved you will not? – Come, come take it or I'll put it up again; for, look ye, I never give more. – Why, how now, mistress, are you so high i'th' mouth, a pistole won't down with you? Hah – why, what a work's here – in good time – come, no struggling to be gone. – But an y'are good at a dumb wrestle, I'm for ye. – Look ye, I'm for ye –

She struggles with him. Enter BELVILE *and* FREDERICK.

BELVILE. The door is open, a pox of this mad fellow, I'm angry that we've lost him, I durst have sworn he had followed us.

FREDERICK. But you were so hasty, Colonel, to be gone.

FLORINDA. Help, help! – Murder! – Help – oh, I am ruined!

BELVILE. Ha, sure, that's Florinda's voice. (*Comes up to them.*) A man! Villain, let go that lady.

A noise. WILLMORE *turns and draws,* FREDERICK *interposes.*

FLORINDA. Belvile! Heavens! My brother, too, is coming, and 'twill be impossible to escape. – Belvile, I conjure you to walk under my chamber-window, from whence I'll give you some instructions what to do. – This rude man has undone us.

Exit.

WILLMORE. Belvile!

Enter PEDRO, STEPHANO, *and other* SERVANTS, *with lights.*

PEDRO. I'm betray'd; run, Stephano, and see if Florinda be safe.

Exit STEPHANO. *They fight and* PEDRO'*s party beats 'em out. Going out, meets* STEPHANO.

So, whoe'er they be, all is not well, I'll to Florinda's chamber.

STEPHANO. You need not, sir, the poor lady's fast asleep and thinks no harm: I would not awake her, sir, for fear of frighting her with your danger.

PEDRO. I'm glad she's there. – Rascals, how came the garden-door open?

STEPHANO. That question comes too late, sir: some of my fellow-servants masquerading I'll warrant.

PEDRO. Masquerading! A lewd custom to debauch our youth – there's something more in this than I imagine.

Exeunt.

Act III, Scene vi

Scene changes to the street. Enter BELVILE *in rage,* FREDERICK *holding him, and* WILLMORE *melancholy.*

WILLMORE. Why, how the devil should I know Florinda?

BELVILE. Ah plague of your ignorance! If it had not been Florinda, must you be a beast? – A brute, a senseless swine?

WILLMORE. Well, sir, you see I am endued with patience –
   I can bear – though egad y'are very free with me methinks –
   I was in good hopes the quarrel would have been on my
   side, for so uncivilly interrupting me.

BELVILE. Peace, brute, whilst thou'rt safe – oh, I'm distracted.

WILLMORE. Nay, nay, I'm an unlucky dog, that's certain.

BELVILE. Ah, curse upon the star that ruled my birth, or whatsoever other influence that makes me still so wretched.

WILLMORE. Thou break'st my heart with these complaints;
   there is no star in fault, no influence but sack, the cursed
   sack I drunk.

FREDERICK. Why, how the devil came you so drunk?

WILLMORE. Why, how the devil came you so sober?

BELVILE. A curse upon his thin skull; he was always beforehand
   that way.

FREDERICK. Prithee, dear Colonel, forgive him, he's sorry for
   his fault.

BELVILE. He's always so after he has done a mischief – a
   plague on all such brutes

WILLMORE. By this light I took her for an arrant harlot.

BELVILE. Damn your debauched opinion; tell me, sot, hadst
   thou so much sense and light about thee to distinguish her
   woman, and couldst not see something about her face and
   person, to strike an awful reverence into thy soul?

WILLMORE. Faith no, I considered her as mere a woman as
   I could wish.

BELVILE. 'Sdeath I have no patience – draw, or I'll kill you.

WILLMORE. Let that alone till to-morrow, and if I set not all
   right again, use your pleasure.

BELVILE To-morrow, damn it.
    The spiteful light will lead me to no happiness.
    To-morrow is Antonio's, and perhaps
    Guides him to my undoing. – Oh that I could meet
    This rival, this powerful fortunate!

WILLMORE. What then?

BELVILE. Let thy own reason, or my rage, instruct thee.

WILLMORE. I shall be finely informed then, no doubt; hear
    me, Colonel – hear me – show me the man and I'll do his
    business.

BELVILE. I know him no more than thou, or if I did, I should
    not need thy aid.

WILLMORE. This you say is Angellica's house, I promised the
    kind baggage to lie with her to-night.

    Offers to go in. Enter ANTONIO *and his page.* ANTONIO *knocks
    on the hilt of his sword.*

ANTONIO. You paid the thousand crowns I directed?

PAGE. To the lady's old woman, sir, I did.

WILLMORE. Who the devil have we here?

BELVILE. I'll now plant myself under Florinda's window, and if
    I find no comfort there, I'll die.

    Exeunt BELVILE *and* FREDERICK. *Enter* MORETTA.

MORETTA. Page!

PAGE. Here's my lord.

WILLMORE. How is this, a picaroon going to board my frigate!
    Here's one chase-gun for you.

    Drawing his sword, jostles ANTONIO *who turns and draws. They
    fight,* ANTONIO *falls.*

MORETTA. Oh, bless us, we're all undone!

Runs in, and shuts the door.

PAGE. Help, murder!

BELVILE *returns at the noise of fighting.*

BELVILE. Ha, the mad rogue's engaged in some unlucky adventure again.

Enter two or three MASQUERADERS.

MASQUERADER. Ha, a man killed!

WILLMORE. How! A man killed! Then I'll go home to sleep.

Puts up, and reels out. Exeunt MASQUERADERS *another way.*

BELVILE. Who should it be? Pray Heaven the rogue is safe, for all my quarrel to him.

As BELVILE *is groping about, enter an* OFFICER *and six* SOLDIERS.

SOLDIER. Who's there?

OFFICER. So, here's one dispatched – secure the murderer.

BELVILE. Do not mistake my charity for murder: I came to his assistance.

SOLDIERS *seize on* BELVILE.

OFFICER. That shall be tried, sir. St Jago, swords drawn in the carnival time!

Goes to ANTONIO.

ANTONIO. Thy hand prithee.

OFFICER. Ha, Don Antonio! Look well to the villain there. – How is it, sir?

ANTONIO. I'm hurt.

BELVILE. Has my humanity made me a criminal?

OFFICER. Away with him.

BELVILE. What a cursed chance is this!

Exeunt SOLDIERS *with* BELVILE.

ANTONIO (*to the* OFFICER). This is the man that has set upon me twice – carry him to my apartment till you have further orders from me.

Exit ANTONIO, *led*.

Act IV, Scene i

A fine room. BELVILE *discover[ed] as by dark alone.*

BELVILE. When shall I be weary of railing on fortune, who is
resolved never to turn with smiles upon me? – Two such
defeats in one night – none but the devil and that mad rogue
could have contrived to have plagued me with – I am here a
prisoner – but where? – Heaven knows – and if there be
murder done, I can soon decide the fate of a stranger in a
nation without mercy. – Yet this is nothing to the torture my
soul bows with, when I think of losing my fair, my dear
Florinda. – Hark – my door opens – a light – a man – and
seems of quality – armed too. – Now shall I die like a dog
without defence.

Enter ANTONIO *in a night-gown, with a light; his arm in a scarf,
and a sword under his arm: he sets the candle on the table.*

ANTONIO. Sir, I come to know what injuries I have done you,
that could provoke you to so mean an action, as to attack
me basely, without allowing time for my defence.

BELVILE. Sir, for a man in my circumstances to plead inno-
cence, would look like fear – but view me well, and you will
find no marks of coward on me, nor anything that betrays
that brutality you accuse me with.

ANTONIO. In vain, sir, you impose upon my sense.
You are not only he who drew on me last night,
But yesterday before the same house, that of Angellica.
Yet there is something in your face and mien
That makes me wish I were mistaken.

BELVILE. I own I fought today in the defence of a friend of
mine, with whom you (if you're the same) and your party,
were first engaged.

Perhaps you think this crime enough to kill me,
But if you do, I cannot fear you'll do it basely.

ANTONIO. No, sir, I'll make you fit for a defence with this.

Gives him the sword.

BELVILE. This gallantry surprises me − nor know I how to use
this present, sir, against a man so brave.

ANTONIO. You shall not need;
For know, I come to snatch you from a danger
That is decreed against you;
Perhaps your life, or long imprisonment:
And 'twas with so much courage you offended,
I cannot see you punished.

BELVILE. How shall I pay this generosity?

ANTONIO. It had been safer to have killed another
Than have attempted me.
To show your danger, sir, I'll let you know my quality:
And 'tis the Viceroy's son whom you have wounded.

BELVILE (*aside*). The Viceroy's son!
Death and confusion! Was this plague reserved
To complete all the rest? (*Aside.*) Obliged by him!
The man of all the world I would destroy.

ANTONIO. You seem disordered, sir.

BELVILE. Yes, trust me, sir, I am, and 'tis with pain
That man receives such bounties,
Who wants the power to pay 'em back again.

ANTONIO. To gallant spirits 'tis indeed uneasy;
− But you may quickly overpay me, sir.

BELVILE (*aside*). Then I am well – kind Heaven! But set
    us even,
That I may fight with him, and keep my honour safe.
[*To* ANTONIO.] Oh, I'm impatient, sir, to be discounting
The mighty debt I owe you; command me quickly –

ANTONIO. I have a quarrel with a rival, sir,
About the maid we love.

BELVILE (*aside*). Death, 'tis Florinda he means –
That thought destroys my reason, and I shall kill him –

ANTONIO. My rival, sir,
Is one has all the virtues man can boast of.

BELVILE (*aside*). Death! Who should this be?

ANTONIO. He challenged me to meet him on the Molo,
As soon as day appear'd; but last night's quarrel
Has made my arm unfit to guide a sword.

BELVILE. I apprehend you, sir, you'd have me kill the man
That lays a claim to the maid you speak of.
– I'll do't – I'll fly to do't!

ANTONIO. Sir, do you know her?

BELVILE. – No, sir, but 'tis enough she is admired by you.

ANTONIO. Sir, I shall rob you of the glory on't,
For you must fight under my name and dress.

BELVILE. That opinion must be strangely obliging that makes
You think I can personate the brave Antonio,
Whom I can but strive to imitate.

ANTONIO. You say too much to my advantage.
Come, sir, the day appears that calls you forth.
Within, sir, is the habit.

Exit ANTONIO.

BELVILE. Fantastic fortune, thou deceitful light,
   That cheats the wearied traveller by night,
   Though on a precipice each step you tread,
   I am resolved to follow where you lead.

   Exit.

Act IV, Scene ii

The Molo. Enter FLORINDA *and* CALLIS *in masks, with*
STEPHANO.

FLORINDA (*aside*). I'm dying with my fears; Belvile's not coming,
   as I expected, under my window, makes me believe that all
   those fears are true. [*To* STEPHANO.] – Canst thou not tell
   with whom my brother fights?

STEPHANO. No, madam, they were both in masquerade, I was
   by when they challenged one another, and they had decided
   the quarrel then, but were prevented by some cavaliers;
   which made 'em put it off till now – but I am sure 'tis about
   you they fight.

FLORINDA (*aside*). Nay then 'tis with Belvile, for what other
   lover have I that dares fight for me, except Antonio? And
   he is too much in favour with my brother. – If it be he, for
   whom shall I direct my prayers to Heaven?

STEPHANO. Madam, I must leave you; for if my master see
   me, I shall be hanged for being your conductor. – I escaped
   narrowly for the excuse I made for you last night i' th'
   garden.

FLORINDA. And I'll reward thee for't – prithee no more.

   Exit STEPHANO. *Enter* DON PEDRO *in his masking habit.*

PEDRO. Antonio's late to-day, the place will fill, and we may be
    prevented.

Walks about.

FLORINDA (*aside*). Antonio? Sure I heard amiss.

PEDRO. But who will not excuse a happy lover.
    When soft, fair arms confine the yielding neck,
    And the kind whisper languishingly breathes,
    Must you be gone so soon?
    Sure I had dwelt for ever on her bosom.
    – But stay, he's here.

Enter BELVILE *dressed in Antonio's clothes.*

FLORINDA (*aside*). 'Tis not Belvile, half my fears are vanished.

PEDRO. Antonio! –

BELVILE (*aside*). This must be he. [*To* PEDRO.] You're early, sir,
    – I do not use to be out-done this way.

PEDRO. The wretched, sir, are watchful, and 'tis enough You've
    the advantage of me in Angellica.

BELVILE (*aside*). Angellica!
    Or I've mistook my man! Or else Antonio,
    Can he forget his interest in Florinda,
    And fight for common prize?

PEDRO. Come, sir, you know our terms.

BELVILE (*aside*). By Heaven, not I!
    [*To* PEDRO.] – No talking, I am ready, sir.

Offers to fight. FLORINDA *runs in.*

FLORINDA (*to* BELVILE). Oh, hold! Whoe'er you be,
        I do conjure you hold!
    If you strike here – I die –

PEDRO. Florinda!

BELVILE. Florinda imploring for my rival!

PEDRO. Away, this kindness is unseasonable.

Puts her by. They fight; she runs in just as BELVILE *disarms* PEDRO.

FLORINDA. Who are you, sir, that dares deny my prayers?

BELVILE. Thy prayers destroy him; if thou wouldst preserve him,
Do that thou'rt unacquainted with, and curse him.

She holds [BELVILE].

FLORINDA. By all you hold most dear, by her you love,
I do conjure you, touch him not.

BELVILE. By her I love!
See – I obey – and at your feet resign
The useless trophy of my victory.

Lays his sword at her feet.

PEDRO. Antonio, you've done enough to prove you love
Florinda.

BELVILE. Love Florinda!
Does Heaven love adoration, pray'r, or penitence?
Love her! Here sir, – your sword again.

Snatches up the sword, and gives it to him.

Upon this truth I'll fight my life away.

PEDRO. No, you've redeemed my sister, and my friendship.

He gives him FLORINDA *and pulls off his vizard to show his face, and puts it on again.*

BELVILE. Don Pedro!

PEDRO. Can you resign your claims to other women,
And give your heart entirely to Florinda?

BELVILE. Entire, as dying saints' confessions are.
    I can delay my happiness no longer.
    This minute, let me make Florinda mine.

PEDRO. This minute let it be – no time so proper,
    This night my father will arrive from Rome,
    And possibly may hinder what we purpose.

FLORINDA. Oh Heavens! This minute!

Enter masqueraders and pass over [the stage].

BELVILE [*aside*]. Oh, do not ruin me!

PEDRO. The place begins to fill; and that we may not be
    observed, do you walk off to St Peter's Church, where I will
    meet you, and conclude your happiness.

BELVILE. I'll meet you there – (*Aside.*) if there be no more saints'
    churches in Naples.

FLORINDA. Oh, stay, sir, and recall your hasty doom:
    Alas, I have not prepared my heart
    To entertain so strange a guest.

PEDRO. Away, this silly modesty is assumed too late.

BELVILE. Heaven, madam! What do you do?

FLORINDA. Do! Despise the man that lays a tyrant's claim.
    To what he ought to conquer by submission.

BELVILE. You do not know me – move a little this way.

Draws her aside.

FLORINDA Yes, you may force me even to the altar,
    But not the holy man that offers there
    Shall force me to be thine.

    PEDRO *talks to* CALLIS *this while.*

BELVILE. Oh, do not lose so blest an opportunity!
    See – 'tis your Belvile – not Antonio,
    Whom your mistaken scorn and anger ruins.

Pulls off his vizard.

FLORINDA Belvile!
Where was my soul it could not meet thy voice,
And take this knowledge in?

As they are talking, enter WILLMORE, *finely dressed, and*
FREDERICK.

WILLMORE No intelligence! No news of Belvile yet – well,
I am the most unlucky rascal in nature – ha! – Am I
deceived – or is it he – look, Fred – 'tis he – my dear
Belvile.

Runs and embraces him. BELVILE's *vizard falls out on's hand.*

BELVILE. Hell and confusion seize thee!

PEDRO. Ha! Belvile! I beg your pardon, sir.

Takes FLORINDA *from him.*

BELVILE. Nay, touch her not. She's mine by conquest, sir;
I won her by my sword.

WILLMORE. Didst thou so – and egad, child, we'll keep her by
the sword.

Draws on PEDRO, BELVILE *goes between [them].*

BELVILE. Stand off.
Thou'rt so profanely lewd, so cursed by Heaven,
All quarrels thou espousest must be fatal.

WILLMORE. Nay, an you be so hot, my valour's coy,
And shall be courted when you want it next.

Puts up his sword.

BELVILE (*to* PEDRO). You know I ought to claim a
victor's right.
But you're the brother to divine Florinda
To whom I'm such a slave – to purchase her,
I durst not hurt the man she holds so dear.

PEDRO. 'Twas by Antonio's, not by Belvile's sword
　　This question should have been decided, sir.
　　I must confess much to your bravery's due,
　　Both now, and when I met you last in arms.
　　But I am nicely punctual in my word,
　　As men of honour ought, and beg your pardon.
　　– For this mistake, another time shall clear.

　　Aside to FLORINDA *as they are going out.*

　　– This was some plot between you and Belvile:
　　But I'll prevent you.

　　[*Exit* PEDRO *and* FLORINDA.]

　　BELVILE *looks after her and begins to walk up and down in rage.*

WILLMORE. Do not be modest now, and lose the woman:
　　but if we shall fetch her back, so –

BELVILE. Do not speak to me.

WILLMORE. Not speak to you! – Egad, I'll speak to you, and
　　will be answered too!

BELVILE. Will you, sir!

WILLMORE. I know I've done some mischief, but I'm so dull
　　a puppy, that I'm the son of a whore, if I know how, or
　　where – prithee inform my understanding. –

BELVILE. Leave me I say, and leave me instantly.

WILLMORE. I will not leave you in this humour, nor till
　　I know my crime.

BELVILE. Death, I'll tell you, sir –

　　Draws and runs at WILLMORE, *he runs out;* BELVILE *after him,*
　　FREDERICK *interposes* [*but remains*].

　　Enter ANGELLICA, MORETTA, *and* SEBASTIAN.

ANGELLICA. Ha – Sebastian – is that not Willmore? Haste,
　　haste, and bring him back.

[*Exit* SEBASTIAN.]

FREDERICK. The Colonel's mad – I never saw him thus before;
I'll after 'em, lest he do some mischief, for I am sure Willmore
will not draw on him.

Exit.

ANGELLICA. I am all rage! My first desires defeated
For one, for aught he knows, that has no
Other merit than her quality,
Her being Don Pedro's sister. – He loves her:
I know 'tis so – dull, dull, insensible –
He will not see me now, though oft invited;
And broke his word last night – false, perjured man!
– He that but yesterday fought for my favours,
And would have made his life a sacrifice
To've gained one night with me,
Must now be hired and courted to my arms.

MORETTA. I told you what would come on't, but Moretta's an
old doting fool. – Why did you give him five hundred
crowns, but to set himself out for other lovers? You should
have kept him poor, if you had meant to have had any good
from him.

ANGELLICA. Oh, name not such mean trifles. Had I given
him all
My youth has earned from sin,
I had not lost a thought nor sigh upon't.
But I have given him my eternal rest,
My whole repose, my future joys, my heart;
My virgin heart. Moretta! Oh 'tis gone!

MORETTA. Curse on him, here he comes;
How fine she has made him, too.

Enter WILLMORE *and* SEBASTIAN. ANGELLICA *turns
and walks away.*

WILLMORE. How now, turned shadow!
Fly when I pursue, and follow when I fly!

Sings.

Stay, gentle shadow of my dove,
    And tell me ere I go,
Whether the substance may not prove
    A fleeting thing like you.

As she turns, she looks on him.

There's a soft, kind look remaining yet.

ANGELLICA. Well, sir, you may be gay: all happiness, all joys
pursue you still, Fortune's your slave and gives you every
hour choice of new hearts and beauties, till you are cloyed
with the repeated bliss, which others vainly languish for. –
But know, false man, that I shall be revenged.

Turns away in rage.

WILLMORE. So, 'gad, there are of those faint-hearted lovers,
whom such a sharp lesson next their hearts would make as
impotent as fourscore – pox o' this whining – my business is
to laugh and love – a pox on't; I hate your sullen lover, a
man shall lose as much time to put you in humour now, as
would serve to gain a new woman.

ANGELLICA. I scorn to cool that fire I cannot raise,
Or do the drudgery of your virtuous mistress.

WILLMORE. A virtuous mistress! Death, what a thing thou
hast found out for me! Why what the devil should I do with a
virtuous woman? – A sort of ill-natured creatures, that take a
pride to torment a lover. Virtue is but an infirmity in woman,
a disease that renders even the handsome ungrateful; whilst
the ill-favoured, for want of solicitations and address, only
fancy themselves so. – I have lain with a woman of quality,
who has all the while been railing at whores.

ANGELLICA. I will not answer for your mistress's virtue,
  Though she be young enough to know no guilt:
  And I could wish you would persuade my heart,
  'Twas the two hundred thousand crowns you courted.

WILLMORE. Two hundred thousand crowns! What story's this?
  – What trick? – What woman? – Ha.

ANGELLICA. How strange you make it! Have you forgot the
  creature you entertained on the Piazza last night?

WILLMORE (*aside*). Ha, my gipsy worth two hundred thousand
  crowns! – Oh, how I long to be with her – pox, I knew she
  was of quality.

ANGELLICA. False man, I see my ruin in thy face.
  How many vows you breathed upon my bosom,
  Never to be unjust – have you forgot so soon?

WILLMORE (*aside*). Faith no, I was just coming to repeat 'em –
  but here's a humour indeed – would make a man a saint. –
  Would she would be angry enough to leave me, and
  command me not to wait on her.

Enter HELLENA, *dressed in man's clothes.*

HELLENA [*aside*]. This must be Angellica, I know it by her
  mumping matron here. – Ay, ay, 'tis she: my mad Captain's
  with her too, for all his swearing – how this unconstant
  humour makes me love him. [*To* MORETTA.] Pray, good
  grave gentlewoman, is not this Angellica?

MORETTA. My too young sir, it is. [*Aside.*] I hope 'tis one from
  Don Antonio.

Goes to ANGELLICA.

HELLENA (*aside*). Well, something I'll do to vex him for this.

ANGELLICA. I will not speak with him; am I in humour to
  receive a lover?

WILLMORE. Not speak with him! Why I'll be gone – and
wait your idler minutes. – Can I show less obedience to the
thing I love so fondly?

Offers to go.

ANGELLICA. A fine excuse this – stay –

WILLMORE. And hinder your advantage: should I repay your
bounties so ungratefully?

ANGELLICA [*to* HELLENA]. Come hither, boy, –
    [*To* WILLMORE.] – that I may let you see
How much above the advantages you name
I prize one minute's joy with you.

WILLMORE (*impatient to be gone*). Oh, you destroy me with
this endearment. – (*Aside.*) Death, how shall I get away?
(*To* ANGELLICA.) Madam, 'twill not be fit I should be seen
with you – besides, it will not be convenient – and I've a
friend – that's dangerously sick.

ANGELLICA. I see you're impatient – yet you shall stay.

WILLMORE (*aside and walks about impatiently*). And miss my
assignation with my gipsy.

   MORETTA *brings* HELLENA, *who addresses herself to*
   ANGELLICA.

HELLENA. Madam,
You'll hardly pardon my intrusion,
When you shall know my business;
And I'm too young to tell my tale with art:
But there must be a wondrous store of goodness
Where so much beauty dwells.

ANGELLICA. A pretty advocate, whoever sent thee. –
Prithee proceed. – (*To* WILLMORE *who is stealing off.*)
    Nay, sir, you shall not go.

WILLMORE (*aside*). Then I shall lose my dear gipsy for ever.
   – Pox on't, she stays me out of spite.

[HELLENA.] I am related to a lady, madam,
   Young, rich, and nobly born, but has the fate
   To be in love with a young English gentleman.
   Strangely she loves him, at first sight she loved him,
   But did adore him when she heard him speak;
   For he, she said, had charms in every word,
   That failed not to surprise, to wound. and conquer –

WILLMORE (*aside*). Ha, egad I hope this concerns me.

ANGELLICA. 'Tis my false man he means – would he were
    gone.
   This praise will raise his pride, and ruin me –
   (*To* WILLMORE.) Well, since you are so impatient to be gone,
   I will release you, sir.

WILLMORE (*aside*). Nay, then I'm sure 'twas me he spoke of, this
   cannot be the effects of kindness in her.

   (*To* ANGELLICA.) – No, madam, I've considered better on't,
   And will not give you cause of jealousy.

ANGELLICA. But, sir, I've – business, that –

WILLMORE. This shall not do, I know 'tis but to try me.

ANGELLICA. Well, to your story, boy, (*Aside.*) though 'twill
    undo me.

HELLENA. With this addition to his other beauties,
   He won her unresisting, tender heart,
   He vowed and sighed, and swore he loved her dearly;
   And she believed the cunning flatterer,
   And thought herself the happiest maid alive:
   To-day was the appointed time by both,
   To consummate their bliss;
   The virgin, altar, and the priest were dressed,

And while she languished for th' expected bridegroom,
She heard, he paid his broken vows to you.

WILLMORE (*aside*). So, this is some dear rogue that's in love
with me, and this way lets me know it; or if it be not me, she
means some one whose place I may supply.

ANGELLICA. Now I perceive
The cause of thy impatience to be gone,
And all the business of this glorious dress.

WILLMORE. Damn the young prater, I know not what he
means.

HELLENA. Madam,
In your fair eyes I read too much concern.
To tell my farther business.

ANGELLICA. Prithee, sweet youth, talk on, thou may'st perhaps
Raise here a storm that may undo my passion,
And then I'll grant thee any thing.

HELLENA. Madam, 'tis to entreat you (oh, unreasonable!)
You would not see this stranger;
For if you do, she vows you are undone,
Though nature never made a man so excellent;
And sure, he'ad been a god, but for inconstancy.

WILLMORE (*aside*). Ah, rogue, how finely he's instructed!
– 'Tis plain some woman that has seen me *en passant.*

ANGELLICA. Oh, I shall burst with jealousy! Do you know the
man you speak of? –

HELLENA. Yes, madam, he used to be in buff and scarlet.

ANGELLICA (*to* WILLMORE). Thou, false as Hell, what canst
thou say to this?

WILLMORE. By Heaven –

ANGELLICA. Hold, do not damn thyself –

HELLENA. Nor hope to be believed.

He walks about, they follow.

ANGELLICA. Oh, perjured man!
Is't thus you pay my generous passion back?

HELLENA. Why would you, sir, abuse my lady's faith?

ANGELLICA. And use me so unhumanely?

HELLENA. A maid so young, so innocent –

WILLMORE. Ah, young devil!

ANGELLICA. Dost thou not know thy life is in my power?

HELLENA. Or think my lady cannot be revenged?

WILLMORE (*aside*). So, so, the storm comes finely on.

ANGELLICA. Now thou art silent, guilt has struck thee dumb.
Oh, hadst thou still been so, I'd lived in safety.

She turns away and weeps.

WILLMORE (*aside to* HELLENA). Sweetheart, the lady's name
and house – quickly: I'm impatient to be with her. –

Looks towards ANGELLICA *to watch her turning; and as she comes
towards them, he meets her.*

HELLENA (*aside*). So now is he for another woman.

WILLMORE. The impudent'st young thing in nature!
I cannot persuade him out of his error, madam.

ANGELLICA. I know he's in the right – yet thou'st a tongue
That would persuade him to deny his faith.

In rage walks away.

WILLMORE (*said softly to* HELLENA). Her name, her name,
dear boy –

HELLENA. Have you forgot it, sir?

WILLMORE (*aside*). Oh, I perceive he's not to know I am a
stranger to his lady. (*To* HELLENA.) – Yes, yes, I do know – but
I have forgot the –

ANGELLICA *turns*.

– By Heaven, such early confidence I never saw.

ANGELLICA. Did I not charge you with this mistress, sir? Which
you denied, though I beheld your perjury.
This little generosity of thine has rendered back my heart.

Walks away.

WILLMORE [*to* HELLENA]. So, you have made sweet work
        here, my little mischief;
Look your lady be kind and good natured now, or
I shall have but a cursed bargain on't.

ANGELLICA *turns towards them*.

(*To* ANGELLICA.) The rogue's bred up to mischief;.
Art thou so great a fool to credit him?

ANGELLICA. Yes, I do; and you in vain impose upon me.
[*To* HELLENA.] – Come hither, boy. – Is not this he you
        spake of?

HELLENA. I think – it is; I cannot swear, but I vow he has just
such another lying lover's look.

HELLENA *looks in his face, he gazes on her*.

WILLMORE (*aside*). Ha! Do not I know that face? –
By Heaven, my little gipsy! What a dull dog was I?
Had I but looked that way, I'd known her.
Are all my hopes of a new woman banished?
– Egad, if I do not fit thee for this, hang me.
[*To* ANGELLICA.] – Madam, I have found out the plot.

HELLENA [*aside*]. Oh lord, what does he say? Am I discovered
        now?

WILLMORE. Do you see this young spark here?

HELLENA [*aside*]. He'll tell her who I am.

WILLMORE. Who do you think this is?

HELLENA [*aside*]. Ay, ay, he does know me. [*To* WILLMORE.] Nay, dear Captain, I am undone if you discover me.

WILLMORE. Nay, nay, no cogging; she shall know what a precious mistress I have.

HELLENA. Will you be such a devil?

WILLMORE. Nay, nay, I'll teach you to spoil sport you will not make. – [*To* ANGELLICA.] This small ambassador comes not from a person of quality, as you imagine, and he says; but from a very arrant gipsy, the talkingst, pratingst, cantingst little animal thou ever saw'st.

ANGELLICA. What news you tell me! That's the thing I mean.

HELLENA (*aside*). Would I were well off the place. – If ever I go a-captain-hunting again. –

WILLMORE. Mean that thing? That gipsy thing? Thou may'st as well be jealous of thy monkey, or parrot as of her: a German motion were worth a dozen of her, and a dream were a better enjoyment, a creature of a constitution fitter for Heaven than man.

HELLENA (*aside*). Though I'm sure he lies, yet this vexes me.

ANGELLICA. You are mistaken, she's a Spanish woman. Made up of no such dull materials.

WILLMORE. Materials! Egad, and she be made of any that will either dispense, or admit of love, I'll be bound to continence.

HELLENA (*aside to him*). Unreasonable man, do you think so?

[WILLMORE] (*to* HELLENA). You may return, my little brazen head, and tell your lady, that till she be handsome enough to be beloved, or I dull enough to be religious, there will be small hopes of me.

ANGELLICA. Did you not promise then to marry her?

WILLMORE. Not I, by Heaven.

ANGELLICA. You cannot undeceive my fears and torments. till you have vowed you will not marry her.

HELLENA (*aside*). If he swears that, he'll be revenged on me indeed for all my rogueries.

ANGELLICA. I know what arguments you'll bring against me, fortune and honour.

WILLMORE. Honour! I tell you, I hate it in your sex; and those that fancy themselves possessed of that foppery, are the most impertinently troublesome of all woman-kind, and will transgress nine commandments to keep one: and to satisfy your jealousy I swear –

HELLENA (*aside to him*). Oh, no swearing, dear Captain –

WILLMORE. If it were possible I should ever be inclined to marry, it should be some kind young sinner, one that has generosity enough to give a favour handsomely to one that can ask it discreetly, one that has wit enough to manage an intrigue of love – oh, how civil such a wench is, to a man that does her the honour to marry her.

ANGELLICA. By Heaven, there's no faith in any thing he says.

Enter SEBASTIAN.

SEBASTIAN. Madam, Don Antonio –

ANGELLICA. Come hither.

HELLENA [*aside*]. Ha, Antonio! He may be coming hither, and he'll certainly discover me, I'll therefore retire without a ceremony.

Exit HELLENA.

ANGELLICA. I'll see him, get my coach ready.

SEBASTIAN. It waits you, madam.

WILLMORE [*aside*]. This is lucky. [*To* ANGELLICA.] What,
   madam, now I may be gone and leave you to the enjoyment
   of my rival?

ANGELLICA. Dull man, that canst not see how ill, how poor,
   That false dissimulation looks – be gone,
   And never let me see thy cozening face again,
   Lest I relapse and kill thee.

WILLMORE. Yes, you can spare me now – farewell till you're
   in better humour – I'm glad of this release – now for my
   gipsy:

   For though to worse we change, yet still we find
   New joys, new charms, in a new miss that's kind.

   Exit.

ANGELLICA. He's gone, and in this ague of my soul
   The shivering fit returns;
   Oh with what willing haste he took his leave,
   As if the longed-for minute were arrived
   Of some blessed assignation.
   In vain I have consulted all my charms,
   In vain this beauty prized, in vain believed
   My eyes could kindle any lasting fires.
   I had forgot my name, my infamy,
   And the reproach that honour lays on those
   That dare pretend a sober passion here.
   Nice reputation, though it leave behind
   More virtues than inhabit where that dwells,
   Yet that once gone, those virtues shine no more.
   – Then since I am not fit to be beloved,
   I am resolved to think on a revenge
   On him that soothed me thus to my undoing.

   Exeunt.

Act IV, Scene iii

A street.

Enter FLORINDA *and* VALERIA *in habits different from what they have been seen in.*

FLORINDA. We're happily escaped, and yet I tremble still.

VALERIA. A lover and fear! Why, I am but half an one, and yet I have courage for any attempt. Would Hellena were here. I would fain have had her as deep in this mischief as we, she'll fare but ill else I doubt.

FLORINDA. She pretended a visit to the Augustine nuns, but I believe some other design carried her out, pray Heavens, we light on her. – Prithee what didst do with Callis?

VALERIA. When I saw no reason would do good on her, I followed her into the wardrobe, and as she was looking for something in a great chest, I toppled her in by the heels, snatched the key of the apartment where you were confined, locked her in, and left her bawling for help.

FLORINDA. 'Tis well you resolve to follow my fortunes, for thou darest never appear at home again after such an action.

VALERIA. That's according as the young stranger and I shall agree. – But to our business – I delivered your letter, your note to Belvile, when I got out under pretence of going to mass, I found him at his lodging, and believe me it came seasonably; for never was man in so desperate a condition. I told him of your resolution of making your escape to-day, if your brother would be absent long enough to permit you; if not, to die rather than be Antonio's.

FLORINDA. Thou should'st have told him I was confined to my chamber upon my brother's suspicion, that the business on the Molo was a plot laid between him and I.

VALERIA. I said all this, and told him your brother was now gone to his devotion, and he resolves to visit every church till he find him; and not only undeceive him in that, but caress him so as shall delay his return home.

FLORINDA. Oh, Heavens! He's here, and Belvile with him too.

They put on their vizards.

Enter DON PEDRO, BELVILE, WILLMORE; BELVILE *and* DON PEDRO *seeming in serious discourse.*

VALERIA. Walk boldly by them, and I'll come at distance, lest he suspect us.

She walks by them and looks back on them.

WILLMORE. Ha! A woman! And of an excellent mien!

PEDRO. She throws a kind look back on you.

WILLMORE. Death, 'tis a likely wench, and that kind look shall not be cast away – I'll follow her.

BELVILE. Prithee do not.

WILLMORE. Do not! By Heavens to the Antipodes, with such an invitation.

[VALERIA] *goes out and* WILLMORE *follows her.*

BELVILE. 'Tis a mad fellow for a wench.

Enter FREDERICK.

FREDERICK. Oh Colonel, such news.

BELVILE. Prithee what?

FREDERICK. News that will make you laugh in spite of fortune.

BELVILE. What, Blunt has had some damned trick put upon him? Cheated, banged, or clapped?

FREDERICK. Cheated sir, rarely cheated of all but his shirt and drawers; the unconscionable whore too turned him out before consummation, so that traversing the streets at midnight, the watch found him in this *fresco*, and conducted him home; by Heaven 'tis such a sight, and yet I durst as well been hanged as laughed at him, or pity him; he beats all that do but ask him a question, and is in such an humour –

PEDRO. Who is't has met with this ill usage, sir?

BELVILE. A friend of ours, whom you must see for mirth's sake. (*Aside.*) I'll employ him to give Florinda time for an escape.

PEDRO. What is he?

BELVILE. A young countryman of ours, one that has been educated at so plentiful a rate, he yet ne'er knew the want of money, and 'twill be a great jest to see how simply he'll look without it. For my part I'll lend him none, and the rogue know not how to put on a borrowing face, and ask first. I'll let him see how good 'tis to play our parts whilst I play his. – Prithee, Fred, do you go home and keep him in that posture till we come.

Exeunt [BELVILE, DON PEDRO, *and* FREDERICK].

Enter FLORINDA *from the farther end of the scene, looking behind her.*

FLORINDA. I am followed still. – Hah – my brother too advancing this way, good Heavens defend me from being seen by him.

She goes off.

Enter WILLMORE, *and after him* VALERIA, *at a little distance.*

WILLMORE. Ah! There she sails, she looks back as she were willing to be boarded, I'll warrant her prize.

He goes out, VALERIA *following.*

Enter HELLENA, *just as he goes out, with a* PAGE.

HELLENA. Hah, is not that my Captain that has a woman in chase? – 'Tis not Angellica. [*To* PAGE.] Boy, follow those people at a distance, and bring me an account where they go in. (*Exit* PAGE.) I'll find his haunts and plague him everywhere. – Ha – my brother!

BELVILE, WILLMORE, PEDRO *cross the stage;* HELLENA *runs off.*

Act IV, Scene iv

Scene changes to another street.

Enter FLORINDA.

FLORINDA. What shall I do, my brother now pursues me. Will no kind power protect me from his tyranny? – Hah, here's a door open, I'll venture in, since nothing can be worse than to fall into his hands, my life and honour are at stake, and my necessity has no choice.

She goes in.

Enter VALERIA, *and* HELLENA'S PAGE *peeping after* FLORINDA.

PAGE. Here she went in, I shall remember this house.

Exit BOY.

VALERIA. This is Belvile's lodging; she's gone in as readily as if she knew it. – Hah – here's that mad fellow again, I dare not venture in – I'll watch my opportunity.

Goes aside.

Enter WILLMORE, *gazing about him.*

WILLMORE. I have lost her hereabouts. – Pox on't she must not scape me so.

Goes out.

Act IV, Scene v

Scene changes to BLUNT'*s chamber, discovers him sitting on a couch in his shirt and drawers, reading.*

BLUNT. So, now my mind's a little at peace, since I have resolved revenge. – A pox on this tailor though, for not bringing home the clothes I bespoke; and a pox of all poor cavaliers, a man can never keep a spare suit for 'em; and I shall have these rogues come in and find me naked; and then I'm undone; but I'm resolved to arm my self – the rascals shall not insult over me too much. (*Puts on an old rusty sword and buff belt.*) – Now, how like a morris-dancer I am equipped – a fine lady-like whore to cheat me thus, without affording me a kindness for my money, a pox light on her, I shall never be reconciled to the sex more, she has made me as faithless as a physician, as uncharitable as a churchman, and as ill-natured as a poet. Oh how I'll use all womankind hereafter! What would I give to have one of 'em within my reach now! Any mortal thing in petticoats, kind fortune, send me; and I'll forgive thy last night's malice. – Here's a cursed book, too (*A Warning to All Young Travellers*) that can instruct me how to prevent such mischief now 'tis too late! Well, 'tis a rare convenient thing to read a little now and then, as well as hawk and hunt.

Sits down again and reads.

Enter to him FLORINDA.

FLORINDA. This house is haunted sure, 'tis well furnished and no living thing inhabits it – hah – a man! Heavens, how he's attired! Sure 'tis some rope-dancer, or fencing master; I tremble now for fear, and yet I must venture now to speak to him. [*To* BLUNT.] Sir, if I may not interrupt your meditations –

He starts up and gazes.

BLUNT. Hah – what's here? Are my wishes granted? And is not that a she creature? 'Adsheartlikins 'tis! What wretched thing art thou – hah!

FLORINDA. Charitable sir, you've told your self already what I am; a very wretched maid, forced by a strange unlucky accident, to seek a safety here, and must be ruined, if you do not grant it.

BLUNT. Ruined! Is there any ruin so inevitable as that which now threatens thee? Dost thou know, miserable woman, into what den of mischiefs thou art fallen? What abyss of confusion? – Hah – dost not see something in my looks that frights thy guilty soul, and makes thee wish to change that shape of woman for any humble animal, or devil? For those were safer for thee, and less mischievous.

FLORINDA. Alas, what mean you, sir? I must confess, your looks have something in 'em makes me fear; but I beseech you, as you seem a gentleman, pity a harmless virgin, that takes your house for sanctuary.

BLUNT. Talk on, talk on, and weep too, till my faith return. Do, flatter me out of my senses again – a harmless virgin with a pox, as much one as t'other, adsheartlikins. Why, what the devil can I not be safe in my house for you? Not in my chamber? Nay, even being naked too cannot secure me. This is an impudence greater than has invaded me yet. – Come, no resistance.

Pulls her rudely.

FLORINDA. Dare you be so cruel?

BLUNT. Cruel, adsheartlikins as a galley slave, or a Spanish whore: cruel, yes, I will kiss and beat thee all over; kiss, and see thee all over; thou shalt lie with me too, not that I care for the enjoyment, but to let thee see I have ta'en deliberated malice to thee, and will be revenged on one whore for the sins of another; I will smile and deceive thee, flatter thee, and beat thee, kiss and swear, and lie to thee, embrace thee and rob thee, as she did me, fawn on thee, and strip thee stark naked; then hang thee out at my window by the heels, with a paper of scurvy verses fastened to thy breast, in praise of damnable women. – Come, come along!

FLORINDA. Alas, sir, must I be sacrificed for the crimes of the most infamous of my sex! I never understood the sins you name.

BLUNT. Do, persuade the fool you love him, or that one of you can be just or honest; tell me I was not an easy coxcomb, or any strange impossible tale: it will be believed sooner than thy false showers or protestations. A generation of damned hypocrites, to flatter my very clothes from my back! Dissembling witches! Are these the returns you make an honest gentleman that trusts, believes, and loves you? – But if I be not even with you – come along, or I shall –

Pulls her again.

Enter FREDERICK.

FREDERICK. Hah, what's here to do?

BLUNT. Adsheartlikins, Fred I am glad thou art come, to be a witness of my dire revenge.

FREDERICK. What's this, a person of quality too, who is upon the ramble to supply the defects of some grave impotent husband?

BLUNT. No, this has another pretence; some very unfortunate accident brought her hither, to save a life pursued by I know not who, or why, and forced to take sanctuary here at Fools' Haven. Adsheartlikins to me of all mankind for protection? Is the ass to be cajoled again, think ye? No, young one, no prayers or tears shall mitigate my rage; therefore prepare for both my pleasures of enjoyment and revenge, for I am resolved to make up my loss here on thy body, I'll take it out in kindness and in beating.

FREDERICK. Now, mistress of mine, what do you think of this?

FLORINDA. I think he will not — dares not be so barbarous.

FREDERICK. Have a care, Blunt, she fetched a deep sigh, she is enamoured with thy shirt and drawers; she'll strip thee even of that. There are, of her calling such unconscionable baggages, and such dexterous thieves, they'll flay a man, and he shall ne'er miss his skin, till he feels the cold. There was a countryman of ours robbed of a row of teeth whilst he was a-sleeping, which the jilt made him buy again when he waked. — [*To* FLORINDA.] You see, lady, how little reason we have to trust you.

BLUNT. 'Dsheartlikins, why, this is most abominable.

FLORINDA. Some such devils there may be, but by all that's holy I am none such, I entered here to save a life in danger.

BLUNT. For no goodness I'll warrant her.

FREDERICK. Faith, damsel, you had e'en confessed the plain truth, for we are fellows not to be caught twice in the same trap. Look on that wreck, a tight vessel when he set out of haven, well-trimmed and laden, and see how a female picaroon of this island of rogues has shattered him, and canst thou hope for any mercy?

BLUNT. No, no, gentlewoman, come along, adsheartlikins we must be better acquainted. — [*To* FREDERICK.] We'll both lie with her, and then let me alone to bang her.

FREDERICK. I'm ready to serve you in matters of revenge, that has a double pleasure in't.

BLUNT. Well said. You hear, little one, how you are condemned by public vote to the bed within, there's no resisting your destiny, sweetheart.

Pulls her.

FLORINDA. Stay, sir, I have seen you with Belvile, an English cavalier, for his sake use me kindly; you know him, sir.

BLUNT. Belvile! Why, yes, sweeting, we do know Belvile, and wish he were with us now, he's a cormorant at whore and bacon, he'd have a limb or two of thee, my virgin pullet: but 'tis no matter. we'll leave him the bones to pick.

FLORINDA. Sir, if you have any esteem for that Belvile, I conjure you to treat me with more gentleness; he'll thank you for the justice.

FREDERICK. Hark ye, Blunt, I doubt we are mistaken in this matter.

FLORINDA. Sir, if you find me not worth Belvile's care, use me as you please; and that you may think I merit better treatment than you threaten – pray take this present –

Gives him a ring: he looks on it.

BLUNT. Hum – a diamond! Why, 'tis a wonderful virtue now that lies in this ring, a mollifying virtue; adsheartlikins there's more persuasive rhetoric in't, than all her sex can utter.

FREDERICK. I begin to suspect something; and 'twould anger us vilely to be trussed up for a rape upon a maid of quality, when we only believe we ruffle a harlot.

BLUNT. Thou art a credulous fellow, but adsheartlikins I have no faith yet; why, my saint prattled as parlously as this does, she gave me a bracelet too, a devil on her: but I sent my man to sell it today for necessaries, and it proved as counterfeit as her vows of love.

FREDERICK. However, let it reprieve her till we see Belvile.

BLUNT. That's hard, yet I will grant it.

Enter a SERVANT.

SERVANT. Oh, sir, the Colonel is just come in with his new friend and a Spaniard of quality, and talks of having you to dinner with 'em.

BLUNT. 'Dsheartlikins, I'm undone – I would not see 'em for the world: hark ye, Fred, lock up the wench in your chamber.

FREDERICK. Fear nothing, madam, whate'er he threatens, you are safe whilst in my hands.

Exeunt FREDERICK *and* FLORINDA.

BLUNT. And, sirrah – upon your life, say – I am not at home – or that I am asleep – or – or anything – away – I'll prevent their coming this way.

Locks the door and exeunt.

Act V, Scene i

Blunt's chamber.

After a great knocking at his chamber door, enter BLUNT *softly, crossing the stage in his shirt and drawers, as before.*

[VOICES] (*call within*). Ned, Ned Blunt, Ned Blunt.

BLUNT. The rogues are up in arms. 'dsheartlikins, this villainous Frederick has betrayed me, they have heard of my blessed fortune.

[VOICES] (*and knocking within*). Ned Blunt, Ned, Ned –

BELVILE [*within*]. Why, he's dead, sir, without dispute dead, he has not been seen to-day; let's break open the door – here – boy –

BLUNT. Ha, break open the door! 'Dsheartlikins that mad fellow will be as good as his word.

BELVILE [*within*]. Boy, bring something to force the door.

A great noise within at the door again.

BLUNT. So, now must I speak in my own defence, I'll try what rhetoric will do – hold – hold, what do you mean, gentlemen, what do you mean?

BELVILE (*within*). Oh rogue, art alive? Prithee open the door, and convince us.

BLUNT. Yes, I am alive, gentlemen – but at present a little busy.

BELVILE (*within*). How! Blunt grown a man of business! Come, come, open, and let's see this miracle.

BLUNT. No, no, no, no, gentlemen, 'tis no great business – but – I am – at – my devotion – 'dsheartlikins, will you not allow a man time to pray?

BELVILE (*within*). Turned religious! A greater wonder than the first, therefore open quickly, or we shall unhinge, we shall.

BLUNT. This won't do. Why, hark ye, Colonel; to tell you the plain truth, I am about a necessary affair of life. – I have a wench with me – you apprehend me? [*Aside.*] The devil's in't if they be so uncivil as to disturb me now.

WILLMORE [*within*]. How, a wench! Nay, then we must enter and partake; no resistance – unless it be your lady of quality, and then we'll keep our distance.

BLUNT [*aside*]. So, the business is out.

WILLMORE [*within*]. Come, come, lend's more hands to the door – now heave all together – (*Breaks open the door.*) so, well done, my boys –

Enter BELVILE, WILLMORE, FREDERICK, PEDRO *and Belvile's* PAGE: BLUNT *looks simply, they all laugh at him, he lays his hand on his sword, and comes up to* WILLMORE.

BLUNT. Hark ye, sir, laugh out your laugh quickly, d'ye hear, and be gone, I shall spoil your sport else; 'dsheartlikins, sir, I shall – the jest has been carried on too long – (*Aside.*) A plague upon my tailor –

WILLMORE. 'Sdeath, how the whore has dressed him! Faith sir, I'm sorry.

BLUNT. Are you so, sir? Keep't to yourself then, sir, I advise you, d'ye hear? For I can as little endure your pity as his mirth.

Lays his hand on's sword.

BELVILE. Indeed, Willmore, thou wert a little too rough with
    Ned Blunt's mistress. Call a person of quality whore, and one
    so young, so handsome, and so eloquent! – Ha, ha, ha.

BLUNT. Hark ye, sir, you know me, and know I can be angry;
    have a care – for 'dsheartlikins I can fight too – I can, sir – do
    you mark me – no more.

BELVILE. Why so peevish, good Ned? Some disappointments,
    I'll warrant – what, did the jealous count her husband return
    just in the nick?

BLUNT. Or the devil, sir – (*They laugh.*) D'ye laugh? Look ye settle
    me a good sober countenance, and that quickly too, or you
    shall know Ned Blunt is not –

BELVILE. Not everybody, we know that.

BLUNT. Not an ass, to be laughed at, sir.

WILLMORE. Unconscionable sinner, to bring a lover so near his
    happiness, a vigorous passionate lover, and then not only cheat
    him of his moveables, but his very desires, too.

BELVILE. Ah, sir, a mistress is a trifle with Blunt; he'll have a
    dozen the next time he looks abroad; his eyes have charms
    not to be resisted: there needs no more than to expose that
    taking person to the view of the fair, and he leads 'em all in
    triumph.

PEDRO. Sir, though I'm a stranger to you, I am ashamed at the
    rudeness of my nation; and could you learn who did it, would
    assist you to make an example of 'em.

BLUNT. Why, ay, there's one speaks sense now, and
    handsomely; and let me tell you gentlemen, I should not
    have showed myself like a jack-pudding, thus to have made
    you mirth, but that I have revenge within my power; for
    know, I have got into my possession a female, who had
    better have fallen under any curse, than the ruin I design
    her: 'dsheartlikins, she assaulted me here in my own

lodgings, and had doubtless committed a rape upon me, had not this sword defended me.

FREDERICK. I know not that, but o' my conscience thou had ravished her, had she not redeemed herself with a ring – let's see it, Blunt.

BLUNT *shows the ring*.

BELVILE [*aside*]. Hah! – The ring I gave Florinda when we exchanged our vows. – Hark ye, Blunt –

Goes to whisper to him.

WILLMORE. No whispering, good Colonel, there's a woman in the case, no whispering.

BELVILE [*to* BLUNT]. Hark ye, fool, be advised, and conceal both the ring and the story, for your reputation's sake; do not let people know what despised cullies we English are: to be cheated and abused by one whore, and another rather bribe thee than be kind to thee, is an infamy to our nation.

WILLMORE. Come, come, where's the wench? We'll see her, let her be what she will, we'll see her.

PEDRO. Ay, ay, let us see her. I can soon discover whether she be of quality, or for your diversion.

BLUNT. She's in Fred's custody.

WILLMORE. Come, come, the key. (*To* FREDERICK, *who gives him the key; they are going.*)

BELVILE. Death! What shall I do? – Stay, gentlemen. – Yet if I hinder 'em, I shall discover all – hold, let's go one at once – give me the key.

WILLMORE. Nay, hold there, Colonel, I'll go first.

FREDERICK. Nay, no dispute, Ned and I have the propriety of her.

WILLMORE. Damn propriety – then we'll draw cuts.

BELVILE *goes to whisper* WILLMORE.

Nay, no corruption, good Colonel: come, the longest sword carries her. –

They all draw, forgetting DON PEDRO, *being a Spaniard, had the longest.*

BLUNT. I yield up my interest to you gentlemen, and that will be revenge sufficient.

WILLMORE (*to* PEDRO). The wench is yours. – [*Aside.*] Pox of his Toledo, I had forgot that.

FREDERICK. Come, sir, I'll conduct you to the lady.

Exeunt FREDERICK *and* PEDRO.

BELVILE (*aside*). To hinder him will certainly discover her. [*To* WILLMORE.] Dost know, dull beast, what mischief thou hast done?

WILLMORE *walking up and down out of humour.*

WILLMORE. Ay, ay, to trust our fortune to lots, a devil on't; 'twas madness, that's the truth on't.

BELVILE. Oh intolerable sot!

Enter FLORINDA, *running, masked,* PEDRO *after her.* WILLMORE *gazing round her.*

FLORINDA (*aside*). Good Heaven, defend me from discovery.

PEDRO. 'Tis but in vain to fly me, you're fallen to my lot.

BELVILE. Sure she's undiscovered yet, but now I fear there is no way to bring her off.

WILLMORE. Why, what a pox is not this my woman, the same I followed but now?

PEDRO *talking to* FLORINDA, *who walks up and down.*

PEDRO. As if I did not know ye, and your business here.

FLORINDA (*aside*). Good Heaven! I fear he does indeed –

PEDRO. Come, pray be kind, I know you meant to be so when you entered here, for these are proper gentlemen.

WILLMORE. But, sir – perhaps the lady will not be imposed upon, she'll choose her man.

PEDRO. I am better bred, than not to leave her choice free.

Enter VALERIA, *and is surprised at sight of* DON PEDRO.

VALERIA (*aside*). Don Pedro here! There's no avoiding him.

FLORINDA (*aside*). Valeria! Then I'm undone –

VALERIA (*to* PEDRO, *running to him*). Oh, have I found you, sir? – The strangest accident – if I had breath – to tell it.

PEDRO. Speak – is Florinda safe? Hellena well?

VALERIA. Ay, ay, sir – Florinda – is safe [*Aside.*] from any fears of you.

PEDRO. Why, where's Florinda? – Speak.

VALERIA. Ay, where indeed, sir? I wish I could inform you – but to hold you no longer in doubt –

FLORINDA (*aside*). Oh, what will she say?

VALERIA. She's fled away in the habit of one of her pages, sir – but Callis thinks you may retrieve her yet, if you make haste away; she'll tell you, sir, the rest – (*Aside.*) if you can find her out.

PEDRO. Dishonourable girl, she has undone my aim – [*To* BELVILE.] Sir – you see my necessity of leaving you, and hope you'll pardon it: my sister, I know, will make her flight to you; and if she do I shall expect she should be rendered back.

BELVILE. I shall consult my love and honour, sir.

Exit PEDRO.

FLORINDA (*to* VALERIA). My dear preserver, let me embrace thee.

WILLMORE. What the devil's all this?

BLUNT. Mystery by this light.

VALERIA. Come, come, make haste and get your selves married quickly, for your brother will return again.

BELVILE. I'm so surprised with fears and joys, so amazed to find you here in safety, I can scarce persuade my heart into a faith of what I see –

WILLMORE. Hark ye, Colonel, is this that mistress who has cost you so many sighs, and me so many quarrels with you?

BELVILE. It is. – (*To* FLORINDA.) Pray give him the honour of your hand.

WILLMORE. Thus it must be received then.

Kneels and kisses her hand.

And with it give your pardon too.

FLORINDA. The friend to Belvile may command me anything.

WILLMORE (*aside*). Death, would I might, 'tis a surprising beauty.

BELVILE. Boy, run and fetch a Father instantly.

Exit BOY.

FREDERICK. So, now do I stand like a dog, and have not a syllable to plead my own cause with: by this hand, madam, I was never thoroughly confounded before, nor shall I ever more dare look up with confidence, till you are pleased to pardon me.

FLORINDA. Sir, I'll be reconciled to you on one condition, that you'll follow the example of your friend, in marrying a maid that does not hate you, and whose fortune (I believe) will not be unwelcome to you.

FREDERICK. Madam, had I no inclinations that way, I should obey your kind commands.

BELVILE. Who, Fred marry; he has so few inclinations for womankind, that had he been possessed of paradise, he might have continued there to this day, if no crime but love could have disinherited him.

FREDERICK. Oh, I do not use to boast of my intrigues.

BELVILE. Boast! Why, thou dost nothing but boast; and I dare swear, wert thou as innocent from the sin of the grape, as thou art from the apple, thou might'st yet claim that right in Eden which our first parents lost by too much loving.

FREDERICK. I wish this lady would think me so modest a man.

VALERIA. She would be sorry then, and not like you half so well, and I should be loath to break my word with you; which was, that if your friend and mine agreed, it should be a match between you and I.

She gives him her hand.

FREDERICK. Bear witness, Colonel, 'tis a bargain.

Kisses her hand.

BLUNT (*to* FLORINDA). I have a pardon to beg too; but adsheartlikins I am so out of countenance, that I'm a dog if I can say any thing to purpose.

FLORINDA. Sir, I heartily forgive you all.

BLUNT. That's nobly said, sweet lady. – Belvile, prithee present her her ring again, for I find I have not courage to approach her myself.

Gives him the ring; [BELVILE] *gives it to* FLORINDA.

Enter BOY.

BOY. Sir, I have brought the Father that you sent for.

BELVILE. 'Tis well, and now my dear Florinda, let's fly to complete that mighty joy we have so long wished and sighed for. – Come, Fred, you'll follow?

FREDERICK. Your example, sir, 'twas ever my ambition in war, and must be so in love.

WILLMORE. And must not I see this juggling knot tied?

BELVILE. No, thou shalt do us better service, and be our guard, lest Don Pedro's sudden return interrupt the ceremony.

WILLMORE. Content; I'll secure this pass.

Exeunt BELVILE, FLORINDA, FREDERICK *and* VALERIA.

Enter BOY.

BOY (*to* WILLMORE). Sir, there's a lady without would speak to you.

WILLMORE. Conduct her in, I dare not quit my post.

BOY [*to* BLUNT]. And sir, your tailor waits you in your chamber.

BLUNT. Some comfort yet, I shall not dance naked at the wedding.

Exeunt BLUNT *and* BOY.

Enter again the BOY, *conducting in* ANGELLICA *in a masking habit and a vizard,* WILLMORE *runs to her.*

WILLMORE. This can be none but my pretty gipsy. – Oh, I see you can follow as well as fly. – Come, confess thyself the most malicious devil in nature, you think you have done my business with Angellica –

ANGELLICA. Stand off, base villain –

She draws a pistol, and holds to his breast.

WILLMORE. Hah, 'tis not she: who art thou? And what's thy business?

ANGELLICA. One thou hast injured, and who comes to kill thee for't.

WILLMORE. What the devil canst thou mean?

ANGELLICA. By all my hopes to kill thee –

Holds still the pistol to his breast, he going back, she following still.

WILLMORE. Prithee on what acquaintance? For I know thee not.

ANGELLICA. Behold this face – so lost to thy remembrance!

Pulls off her vizard.

And then call all thy sins about thy soul,
And let 'em die with thee.

WILLMORE. Angellica!

ANGELLICA. Yes, traitor,
Does not thy guilty blood run shivering through thy veins?
Hast thou no horror at this sight, that tells thee,
Thou hast not long to boast thy shameful conquest?

WILLMORE. Faith, no child, my blood keeps its old ebbs and flows still, and that usual heat too, that could oblige thee with a kindness, had I but opportunity.

ANGELLICA. Devil! Dost wanton with my pain – have at thy heart.

WILLMORE. Hold, dear virago! Hold thy hand a little,
I am not now at leisure to be killed – hold and hear me –
(*Aside.*) Death, I think she's in earnest.

ANGELLICA (*aside, turning from him*). Oh if I take not heed,
My coward heart will leave me to his mercy.
[*To* WILLMORE.] – What have you, sir, to say? – But
should I hear thee,
Thou'ldst talk away all that is brave about me:

Follows him with the pistol to his breast.

And I have vowed thy death, by all that's sacred.

WILLMORE. Why then there's an end of a proper handsome
fellow, that might 'a lived to have done good service yet:
that's all I can say to't.

ANGELLICA (*pausingly*). Yet – I would give thee – time for
penitence.

WILLMORE. Faith, child, I thank God I have ever took care to
lead a good, sober, hopeful life, and am of a religion that
teaches me to believe I shall depart in peace.

ANGELLICA. So will the devil: tell me
How many poor believing fools thou hast undone;
How many hearts thou hast betrayed to ruin!
– Yet these are little mischiefs to the ills
Thou'st taught mine to commit: thou'st taught it love!

WILLMORE. Egad, 'twas shrewdly hurt the while.

ANGELLICA. – Love, that has robbed it of its unconcern,
Of all that pride that taught me how to value it.
And in its room a mean submissive passion was conveyed,
That made me humbly bow, which I ne'er did
To any thing but Heaven.
– Thou, perjured man, didst this, and with thy oaths,
Which on thy knees thou didst devoutly make,
Softened my yielding heart – and then, I was a slave –
Yet still had been content to've worn my chains,
Worn 'em with vanity and joy for ever,
Hadst thou not broke those vows that put them on.
– 'Twas then I was undone.

All this while follows him with the pistol to his breast.

WILLMORE. Broke my vows! Why, where hast thou lived?
Amongst the gods! For I never heard of mortal man,
That has not broke a thousand vows.

ANGELLICA. Oh, impudence!

WILLMORE. Angellica! That beauty has been too long tempting.
Not to have made a thousand lovers languish,
Who in the amorous favour, no doubt have sworn
Like me; did they all die in that faith? Still adoring?
I do not think they did.

ANGELLICA. No, faithless man: had I repaid their vows, as
I did thine, I would have killed the ingrateful that had
abandoned me.

WILLMORE. This old General has quite spoiled thee, nothing
makes a woman so vain, as being flattered; your old lover
ever supplies the defects of age, with intolerable dotage, vast
charge, and that which you call constancy; and attributing
all this to your own merits, you domineer, and throw your
favours in's teeth, upbraiding him still with the defects of
age, and cuckold him as often as he deceives your
expectations. But the gay, young, brisk lover, that brings his
equal fires, and can give you dart for dart, you'll find will be
as nice as you sometimes.

ANGELLICA. All this thou'st made me know, for which
I hate thee.
Had I remained in innocent security,
I should have thought all men were born my slaves;
And worn my power like lightning in my eyes,
To have destroyed at pleasure when offended.
– But when love held the mirror, the undeceiving glass
Reflected all the weakness of my soul, and made me know,
My richest treasure being lost, my honour,
All the remaining spoil could not be worth

The conqueror's care or value.
– Oh how I fell like a long worshipped idol,
Discovering all the cheat!
Would not the incense and rich sacrifice,
Which blind devotion offered at my altars,
Have fallen to thee?
Why would'st thou then destroy my fancied power?

WILLMORE. By Heaven, thou'rt brave, and I admire thee
    strangely.
I wish I were that dull, that constant thing,
Which thou would'st have, and nature never meant me:
I must, like cheerful birds, sing in all groves,
And perch on every bough,
Billing the next kind she that flies to meet me;
Yet after all could build my nest with thee,
Thither repairing when I'd loved my round,
And still reserve a tributary flame.
– To gain your credit, I'll pay you back your charity,
And be obliged for nothing but for love.

Offers her a purse of gold.

ANGELLICA. Oh, that thou wert in earnest!
So mean a thought of me,
Would turn my rage to scorn, and I should pity thee,
And give thee leave to live;
Which for the public safety of our sex,
And my own private injuries, I dare not do.
Prepare –

Follows still, as before.

– I will no more be tempted with replies.

WILLMORE. Sure –

ANGELLICA. Another word will damn thee! I've heard thee talk
    too long.

She follows him with the pistol ready to shoot: he retires, still amazed.
Enter DON ANTONIO, *his arm in a scarf, and lays hold on the*
pistol.

ANTONIO. Hah! Angellica!

ANGELLICA. Antonio! What devil brought thee hither?

ANTONIO. Love and curiosity, seeing your coach at door.
  Let me disarm you of this unbecoming instrument of death.
  (*Takes away the pistol.*) Amongst the number of your slaves, was
  there not one worthy the honour to have fought your
  quarrel? [*To* WILLMORE.] – Who are you, sir, that are so
  very wretched to merit death from her?

WILLMORE. One, sir, that could have made a better end of an
  amorous quarrel without you, than with you.

ANTONIO. Sure, 'tis some rival – hah – the very man took
  down her picture yesterday – the very same that set on me
  last night – blest opportunity –

Offers to shoot him.

ANGELLICA. Hold, you're mistaken, sir.

ANTONIO. By Heaven, the very same!
  – Sir, what pretensions have you to this lady?

WILLMORE. Sir, I do not use to be examined, and am ill at
  all disputes but this –

Draws, ANTONIO *offers to shoot.*

ANGELLICA (*to* WILLMORE). Oh, hold! You see he's armed
  with certain death:
  – And you, Antonio, I command you hold,
  By all the passion you've so lately vowed me.

Enter DON PEDRO, *sees* ANTONIO, *and stays*.

PEDRO (*aside*). Hah, Antonio! And Angellica!

ANTONIO. When I refuse obedience to your will,
    May you destroy me with your mortal hate.
    By all that's holy I adore you so,
    That even my rival, who has charms enough
    To make him fall a victim to my jealousy,
    Shall live, nay, and have leave to love on still.

PEDRO (*aside*). What's this I hear?

ANGELLICA (*pointing to* WILLMORE). Ah, thus, 'twas thus
        he talked, and I believed.
    – Antonio, yesterday,
    I'd not have sold my interest in his heart,
    For all the sword has won and lost in battle.
    – But now to show my utmost of contempt,
    I give thee life – which if thou would'st preserve,
    Live where my eyes may never see thee more,
    Live to undo someone, whose soul may prove
    So bravely constant to revenge my love.

    Goes out, ANTONIO *follows, but* PEDRO *pulls him back.*

PEDRO. Antonio – stay.

ANTONIO. Don Pedro –

PEDRO. What coward fear was that prevented thee
    From meeting me this morning on the Molo?

ANTONIO. Meet thee?

PEDRO. Yes me; I was the man that dared thee to't.

ANTONIO. Hast thou so often seen me fight in war,
    To find no better cause to excuse my absence?
    – I sent my sword and one to do thee right,
    Finding myself uncapable to use a sword.

PEDRO. But 'twas Florinda's quarrel that we fought,
    And you to show how little you esteemed her,
    Sent me your rival, giving him your interest.

– But I have found the cause of this affront,
And when I meet you fit for the dispute,
– I'll tell you my resentment.

ANTONIO. I shall be ready, sir, ere long to do you reason.

Exit ANTONIO.

PEDRO. If I could find Florinda, now whilst my anger's high,
I think I should be kind, and give her to Belvile in revenge.

WILLMORE. Faith, sir, I know not what you would do, but
I believe the priest within has been so kind.

PEDRO. How! My sister married?

WILLMORE. I hope by this time she is, and bedded too, or he
has not my longings about him.

PEDRO. Dares he do this? Does he not fear my power?

WILLMORE. Faith not at all. If you will go in, and thank him
for the favour he has done your sister, so; if not, sir, my
power's greater in this house than yours; I have a damned
surly crew here, that will keep you till the next tide, and then
clap you on board for prize; my ship lies but a league off the
Molo, and we shall show your Donship a damned
Tramontana rover's trick.

Enter BELVILE.

BELVILE. This rogue's in some new mischief – hah, Pedro
returned!

PEDRO. Colonel Belvile, I hear you have married my sister.

BELVILE You have heard truth then, sir.

PEDRO. Have I so? Then, sir, I wish you joy.

BELVILE. How!

PEDRO. By this embrace I do, and I am glad on't.

BELVILE Are you in earnest?

PEDRO. By our long friendship and my obligations to thee, I am. The sudden change I'll give you reasons for anon. Come, lead me to my sister, that she may know I now approve her choice.

Exit BELVILE *with* PEDRO. WILLMORE *goes to follow them. Enter* HELLENA *as before in boy's clothes, and pulls him back.*

WILLMORE. Ha! My gipsy – now a thousand blessings on thee for this kindness. Egad, child, I was e'en in despair of ever seeing thee again; my friends are all provided for within, each man his kind woman.

HELLENA. Hah! I thought they had served me some such trick.

WILLMORE. And I was e'en resolved to go abroad, condemn myself to my lone cabin, and the thoughts of thee.

HELLENA. And could you have left me behind? Would you have been so ill-natured?

WILLMORE. Why, 'twould have broke my heart, child – but since we are met again, I defy foul weather to part us.

HELLENA. And would you be a faithful friend now, if a maid should trust you?

WILLMORE. For a friend I cannot promise, thou art of a form so excellent, a face and humour too good for cold dull friendship; I am parlously afraid of being in love, child, and you have not forgot how severely you have used me.

HELLENA. That's all one, such usage you must still look for, to find out all your haunts, to rail at you to all that love you, till I have made you love only me in your own defence, because nobody else will love you.

WILLMORE. But hast thou no better quality to recommend thyself by?

HELLENA. Faith none, Captain – why, 'twill be the greater charity to take me for thy mistress, I am a lone child, a kind

of orphan lover; and why I should die a maid, and in a
Captain's hands too, I do not understand.

WILLMORE. Egad, I was never clawed away with broadsides
from any female before, thou hast one virtue I adore, good
nature; I hate a coy demure mistress, she's as troublesome as
a colt, I'll break none; no, give me a mad mistress when
mewed, and in flying one I dare trust upon the wing, that
whilst she's kind will come to the lure.

HELLENA. Nay, as kind as you will, good Captain, whilst it
lasts, but let's lose no time.

WILLMORE. My time's as precious to me, as thine can be;
therefore, dear creature, since we are so well agreed, let's
retire to my chamber, and if ever thou wert treated with
such savoury love. – Come – my bed's prepared for such a
guest, all clean and sweet as thy fair self; I love to steal a
dish and a bottle with a friend, and hate long graces. –
Come, let's retire and fall to.

HELLENA. 'Tis but getting my consent, and the business is
soon done; let but old Gaffer Hymen and his priest say
Amen to't, and I dare lay my mother's daughter by as
proper a fellow as your father's son, without fear or blushing.

WILLMORE. Hold, hold, no bug words, child, priest and
Hymen: prithee add a hangman to 'em to make up the
consort. – No, no, we'll have no vows but love, child, nor
witness but the lover; the kind deity enjoins naught but love
and enjoy. Hymen and priest wait still upon portion, and
jointure; love and beauty have their own ceremonies.
Marriage is as certain a bane to love, as lending money is to
friendship: I'll neither ask nor give a vow, though I could be
content to turn gipsy, and become a left-handed bridegroom,
to have the pleasure of working that great miracle of making
a maid a mother, if you durst venture; 'tis upse gipsy that,
and if I miss, I'll lose my labour.

HELLENA. And if you do not lose, what shall I get? A cradle full of noise and mischief, with a pack of repentance at my back? Can you teach me to weave incle to pass my time with? 'Tis upse gipsy that, too.

WILLMORE. I can teach thee to weave a true love's knot better.

HELLENA. So can my dog.

WILLMORE. Well, I see we are both upon our guards, and I see there's no way to conquer good nature, but by yielding – here – give me thy hand – one kiss and I am thine –

HELLENA. One kiss! How like my page he speaks; I am resolved you shall have none, for asking such a sneaking sum. – He that will be satisfied with one kiss, will never die of that longing; good friend single-kiss, is all your talking come to this? A kiss, a caudle! Farewell Captain Single-Kiss.

Going out he stays her.

WILLMORE. Nay, if we part so, let me die like a bird upon a bough, at the sheriff's charge. By Heaven, both the Indies shall not buy thee from me. I adore thy humour and will marry thee, and we are so of one humour, it must be a bargain – give me thy hand – (*Kisses her hand.*) and now let the blind ones (love and fortune) do their worst.

HELLENA. Why, God-a-mercy, Captain!

WILLMORE. But hark ye – the bargain is now made; but is it not fit we should know each other's names? That when we have reason to curse one another hereafter, and people ask me who 'tis I give to the devil, I may at least be able to tell what family you came of.

HELLENA. Good reason, Captain; and where I have cause (as I doubt not but I shall have plentiful) that I may know at whom to throw my – blessings – I beseech ye your name.

WILLMORE. I am called Robert the Constant.

HELLENA. A very fine name! Pray was it your falconer or butler that christened you? Do they not use to whistle when they call you?

WILLMORE. I hope you have a better, that a man may name without crossing himself, you are so merry with mine.

HELLENA. I am called Hellena the Inconstant.

Enter PEDRO, BELVILE, FLORINDA, FREDERICK, VALERIA.

PEDRO. Hah! Hellena!

FLORINDA. Hellena!

HELLENA. The very same – hah my brother! Now, Captain, show your love and courage; stand to your arms, and defend me bravely, or I am lost for ever.

PEDRO. What's this I hear? False girl, how came you hither, and what's your business? Speak.

Goes roughly to her.

WILLMORE. Hold off, sir, you have leave to parley only.

Puts himself between.

HELLENA. I had e'en as good tell it, as you guess it. Faith, brother, my business is the same with all living creatures of my age, to love and be beloved, and here's the man.

PEDRO. Perfidious maid, hast thou deceived me too, deceived thy self and Heaven?

HELLENA. 'Tis time enough to make my peace with that, Be you but kind, let me alone with Heaven.

PEDRO. Belvile, I did not expect this false play from you; was't not enough you'd gain Florinda (which I pardoned) but your lewd friends too must be enriched with the spoils of a noble family?

BELVILE. Faith, sir, I am as much surprised at this as you can
be: yet, sir, my friends are gentlemen, and ought to be
esteemed for their misfortunes, since they have the glory to
suffer with the best of men and kings; 'tis true, he's a rover of
fortune, yet a prince aboard his little wooden world.

PEDRO. What's this to the maintenance of a woman of her
birth and quality?

WILLMORE. Faith, sir, I can boast of nothing but a sword
which does me right where'er I come, and has defended a
worse cause than a woman's: and since I loved her before I
either knew her birth or name, I must pursue my resolution,
and marry her.

PEDRO [to HELLENA]. And is all your holy intent of becoming
a nun debauched into a desire of man?

HELLENA. Why – I have considered the matter, brother, and
find the three hundred thousand crowns my uncle left me
(and you cannot keep from me) will be better laid out in love
than in religion, and turn to as good an account – let most
voices carry it, for Heaven or the Captain?

ALL (cry). A Captain, a Captain!

HELLENA. Look ye, sir, 'tis a clear case.

PEDRO. Oh I am mad – (Aside.) if I refuse, my life's in danger.
[To WILLMORE.] – Come – there's one motive induces
me – take her – I shall now be free from fears of her
honour; guard it you now, if you can, I have been a slave
to't long enough.

Gives her to him.

WILLMORE. Faith, sir, I am of a nation that are of opinion a
woman's honour is not worth guarding when she has a mind
to part with it.

HELLENA. Well said, Captain.

PEDRO (*to* VALERIA). This was your plot, mistress, but I hope you have married one that will revenge my quarrel to you –

VALERIA. There's no altering destiny, sir.

PEDRO. Sooner than a woman's will, therefore I forgive you all – and wish you may get my father's pardon as easily; which I fear.

Enter BLUNT *dressed in a Spanish habit, looking very ridiculously; his* MAN *adjusting his band.*

MAN. 'Tis very well, sir.

BLUNT. Well, sir, 'dsheartlikins I tell you 'tis damnable ill, sir – a Spanish habit, good Lord! Could the devil and my tailor devise no other punishment for me, but the mode of a nation I abominate?

BELVILE. What's the matter, Ned?

BLUNT. Pray view me round and judge.

Turns round.

BELVILE. I must confess thou art a kind of an odd figure.

BLUNT. In a Spanish habit with a vengeance! I had rather be in the Inquisition for Judaism, than in this doublet and breeches; a pillory were an easy collar to this, three handfuls high; and these shoes too are worse than the stocks, with the sole an inch shorter than my foot. In fine, gentlemen, methinks I look altogether like a bag of bays stuffed full of fool's flesh.

BELVILE. Methinks 'tis well, and makes theè look *en cavalier*. Come, sir, settle your face, and salute our friends. Lady –

BLUNT (*to* HELLENA). Hah! Say'st thou so, my little rover? Lady – (if you be one) give me leave to kiss your hand, and tell you, adsheartlikins, for all I look so, I am your humble servant. – A pox of my Spanish habit!

Music is heard to play.

WILLMORE. Hark – what's this?

Enter BOY.

BOY. Sir, as the custom is, the gay people in masquerade, who make every man's house their own, are coming up.

Enter several men and women in masking habits, with music. They put themselves in order and dance.

BLUNT. Adsheartlikins, would 'twere lawful to pull off their false faces, that I might see if my doxy were not amongst 'em.

BELVILE (*to the* MASKERS). Ladies and gentlemen, since you are come so apropos, you must take a small collation with us.

WILLMORE (*to* HELLENA). Whilst we'll to the good man within, who stays to give us a cast of his office. – Have you no trembling at the near approach?

HELLENA. No more than you have in an engagement or a tempest.

WILLMORE. Egad, thou'rt a brave girl, and I admire thy love and courage.

Lead on, no other dangers they can dread,
Who venture in the storms o' th' marriage bed.

Exeunt.

Epilogue

The banished cavaliers! A roving blade!
A popish carnival! A masquerade!
The devil's in't if this will please the nation,
In these our blessed times of reformation,
When conventicling is so much in fashion.
And yet –
That mutinous tribe less factions do beget,
Than your continual differing in wit;
Your judgement's (as your passion's) a disease:
Nor muse nor miss your appetite can please;
You're grown as nice as queasy consciences,
Whose each convulsion, when the spirit moves,
Damns everything that maggot disapproves.

With canting rule you would the stage refine,
And to dull method all our sense confine.
With th' insolence of commonwealths you rule,
Where each gay fop, and politic grave fool
On monarch wit impose without control.
As for the last who seldom sees a play,
Unless it be the old Blackfriars way,
Shaking his empty noddle o'er bamboo,
He cries, 'Good faith, these plays will never do.
– Ah, sir, in my young days, what lofty wit,
What high-strained scenes of fighting there were writ:
These are slight airy toys. But tell me, pray,
What has the House of Commons done today?'
Then shows his politics, to let you see

Of state affairs he'll judge as notably,
As he can do of wit and poetry.

The younger sparks, who hither do resort,
Cry, 'Pox o' your genteel things. Give us more sport;
– Damn me, I'm sure 'twill never please the court.'

Such fops are never pleased, unless the play
Be stuffed with fools, as brisk and dull as they:
Such might the half-crown spare, and in a glass
At home behold a more accomplished ass,
Where they may set their cravats, wigs and faces,
And practise all their buffoonery grimaces;
See how this – huff becomes – this damme – stare,
Which they at home may act, because they dare,
But – must with prudent caution do elsewhere.
Oh that our Nokes, or Tony Lee, could show
A fop but half so much to th' life as you.

Postscript

This play had been sooner in print, but for a report about the town (made by some either very malicious or very ignorant) that 'twas *Thomaso* altered; which made the booksellers fear some trouble from the proprietor of that admirable play, which indeed has wit enough to stock a poet, and is not to be pieced or mended by any but the excellent author himself. That I have stolen some hints from it may be a proof, that I valued it more than to pretend to alter it: had I had the dexterity of some poets who are not more expert in stealing than in the art of concealing, and who even that way outdo the Spartan-boys I might have appropriated all to myself, but I, vainly proud of my judgement, hang out the sign of Angellica (the only stolen object) to give notice where a great part of the wit dwelt; though if the play of *The Novella* were as well worth remembering as *Thomaso,* they might (bating the name) have as well said, I took it from thence: I will only say the plot and business (not to boast on't) is my own: as for the words and characters, I leave the reader to judge and compare 'em with *Thomaso,* to whom I recommend the great entertainment of reading it, though had this succeeded ill, I should have had no need of imploring that justice from the critics, who are naturally so kind to any that pretend to usurp their dominion, especially of our sex, they would doubtless have given me the whole honour on't. Therefore I will only say in English what the famous Virgil does in Latin: I make verses, and others have the fame.

Glossary

adsheartlikins, *'sheartlikins* – abbreviated forms of 'God's heartlikins', or 'God's little heart', a term of affection, here used simply as an exclamation or catch-phrase by Blunt

apropos – opportunely, in timely fashion

bamboo – cane walking-stick

bating – other than

black-lead – pencil

Blackfriars way – ie, in the style of plays seen at the former Blackfriars playhouse, now regarded as old-fashioned

bona roba – a good (but often showy) dresser

broadsides – in V, i, a sustained artillery attack from one side of a vessel

cabal – political or literary faction

Capuchin – hooded friar

Carnival – here, specifically the brief period of celebration immediately preceding the deprivations of Lent

cast, venture a – take a risk (as in throwing dice)

cast of his office – a sign of his role: in the priest's case, to perform a marriage

caudle – warm gruel

chapmen – strolling dealers in cheap goods (sometimes, also their customers)

cits – citizens, specifically (often derogatorily) of the City of London

clap, proclaimed – visible signs of venereal disease

Commonwealth – here, specifically the period of republican rule, from 1649 to 1653

conventicling – going to meetings (conventicles) of religious dissenters

Damon − rustic shepherd and lover

Essex − then as now a target for Londoners' derogatory jokes

extempore, mimic good − to imitate verse which better poets can make up as they go along

Father − in V, i, a priest (to perform the marriage)

Flanders − Spanish possession in the Netherlands, lost to French incursions

fresco, in − in the open (fresh) air

grate − in I, i, the barred window between a nun and the outside world

hogoes − well-flavoured relishes

humour, hit your − caricature you accurately

incle − linen thread

Infanta, portion for the − dowry fit for the Spanish King's daughter

Jephthah's daughter − in the biblical Book of Judges, a daughter condemned to be sacrificed by her own father, but first permitted to bemoan her virgin state

Lee, Tony − contemporary comic actor

Loretto, road to − well-travelled road (leading to a place of pilgrimage on the Adriatic)

maggot − here, contemptuous reference to the inner spiritual voice heeded by religious dissenters

mewed − shut up, restrained

Molo − stone-built pier

motion − puppet (ie, lifeless)

mutinous tribe − ie, religious dissenters, nonconformists

name, forgot my − failed to consider my reputation

New Bridge − Nieuwerbrug: Dutch garrison which fell to the French in 1672 (the reference here thus being anachronistic)

Nokes − contemporary comic actor

Novella, The − comedy by Richard Brome (1632)

Pamplona − Northern Spanish town, guarding a pass through the Pyrenees (in besieging which Belvile served as a mercenary for the French army)

Piazza − open square

picaroon − wanderer, often piratical

Prado – promenade, place of fashionable assembly

Prince, the – at I, ii, specifically the exiled Prince Charles, later Charles II

propriety – rightful ownership

quean – hussy

Rabel's drops – a quack medicine

'sheartlikins – see *adsheartlikins*

shore, common – public sewer

sybil – classical prophetess

Thomaso – play by Thomas Killigrew, alleged to have been plagiarised by Behn for *The Rover*

Toledo – Spanish sword, long and finely-honed

Tramontana – from over the mountains; hence, in Italy, anything to (or from) the north of the Alps

upse gispsy – like a gipsy; gipsy-style

ycleped – known as, called